DARREN FLEMING

MINDSET MASTERY
Do less. Achieve more.

'Better integrating all aspects of your life (work, family, community and self) is a wicked challenge. Essential to meeting that is presence. Darren's insight is how to achieve mindfulness by bringing calm and peace to the blooming, buzzing miasma of thoughts racing in our heads. Want a better work-life? Best read Darren.'

Professor Clive Smallman, Kingsford Institute of Higher Education, International Institute for MBA Studies

'Darren's *Mindset Mastery* codifies a simple tool to help complex problems so it's instantly usable. If you are struggling to put down distress or make a decision, this book could be your answer.'

Dr Amy Silver ClinPysD MPhil MA BSc(Hons), author of **The Loudest Guest: How to change and control your relationship with fear**

'There is a lot of science around proving that being present, living mindfully, and mastering our mindset has enormous benefits. Benefits for productivity, relationships, happiness, wellbeing and more. This is an easy-to-read, compelling step-by-step guide for how to master your mindset. Highly recommended for anyone who wants to get better at anything.'

Peter Cook, Author, Monk, Entrepreneur

'Mastering your mindset makes the difference between bringing out your "good" performance and bringing out your "A game". *Mindset Mastery* is a powerful key that will allow you to realise your full potential.'

Michael Bradburn, CFO, Ultra-marathon runner

'Darren Fleming has written a must-read guide for anyone wanting to be free of any limitations to their success. He teaches us a simple-to-follow, extremely effective technique to overcome inner tension, addictive behaviours, fear and cravings so that we can go on to live our best life.'

Alessandra Edwards, Performance expert and genetic strategist

'New thinking in the behaviour change and leadership space is rare, but Darren has done it. Darren's insights give us a step-by-step process to deactivate why we think the way we do and how to think differently. A must-read for everyone.'

Justin McNeany, Director, Keynote Entertainers talent and celebrity management

'What I love about Darren's work is that he combines psychological science with Eastern wisdom and no-nonsense performance practicality. In Darren's hands, Mindset Mastery is a sound practice and skill that is anything but soft. Highly recommended!'

Dan Gregory, Speaker, Author, Social Commentator, Comedian, Behavioural Trends & Strategy

'We've all made the same mistake over and over, without knowing why, or what to do about it. In *Mindset Mastery*, Darren unpacks why this happens, and shows us how to avoid it in the future. Simple, straightforward and genuinely funny, *Mindset Mastery* is for everyone.'

Thomas Preiss, Sales Performance Coach, Advisor and Facilitator

Dedication

For Alice and Addie who opened the door
and invited me to learn this.
To Ali who guided me along the path.
Thank you.

First published in 2023 by Darren Fleming

© Darren Fleming 2023
The moral rights of the author have been asserted

All rights reserved. Except as permitted under the *Australian Copyright Act 1968* (for example, a fair dealing for the purposes of study, research, criticism or review), no part of this book may be reproduced, stored in a retrieval system, communicated or transmitted in any form or by any means without prior written permission.

All inquiries should be made to the author.

A catalogue entry for this book is available from the National Library of Australia.

ISBN: 978-0-9944098-2-9

Printed in Australia by McPherson's Printing
Book production and text design by Publish Central
Cover design by Dan Gregory

The paper this book is printed on is certified as environmentally friendly.

Disclaimer: The material in this publication is of the nature of general comment only, and does not represent professional advice. It is not intended to provide specific guidance for particular circumstances and it should not be relied on as the basis for any decision to take action or not take action on any matter which it covers. Readers should obtain professional advice where appropriate, before making any such decision. To the maximum extent permitted by law, the author and publisher disclaim all responsibility and liability to any person, arising directly or indirectly from any person taking or not taking action based on the information in this publication.

CONTENTS

Preface: We're prisoners of habit: life without
Mindset Mastery ... xi

PART I: HOW WE INTERACT WITH THE WORLD ... XIX

Chapter 1: Understanding your programming ... 1

    Equanimity: the secret to Mindset Mastery ... 4
    Understanding and mastering our reactions ... 5
    All life is suffering ... 9
    How to become non-attached ... 12
    How this affects us day to day ... 14

Chapter 2: Energy is everything ... 17

    The atoms inside you ... 18
    Common but unproductive ways of dealing
        with sensations ... 21
    Why we don't feel the energy in our body ... 22
    A word on labelling ... 24
    Habituation ... 25
    How to observe sensations ... 26
    What to look for ... 27
    What this gives you ... 30

Chapter 3: The voice in your head — 31

    That complete jerk that tries to derail us — 33
    Thoughts from sensations — 38
    Spotting when you are in the grip of the voice — 39
    Talking to itself — 41
    How to deactivate unwanted thoughts — 42

Chapter 4: It's all a story — 43

    The world is an inkblot — 45
    The meaning we project — 46
    The value of our made-up stories — 47
    Sensations and stories — 50
    How this plays out — 54

PART II: MINDSET MASTERY IN ACTION — 57

Chapter 5: The power of doing nothing — 59

    Doing nothing — 61
    The four ways we don't do nothing — 63
    Do nothing in all areas of life — 68
    How to do nothing — 70
    The *Six Don'ts* — 71
    Holding down the volcano — 74
    What if you don't do nothing? — 75

Chapter 6: Putting Mindset Mastery to work — 79

    The $25,000 mind technique — 80
    A quick calibration — 84
    Overcoming imposter syndrome — 85
    Making sales calls — 86
    That person who pisses you off — 88

That drink when I get home	89
Making money work	91
Drop 20 kilos	94
Back to sleep at 3 am	95
Chocolate be gone	96
Men in Black – memory erasing	98
You 2.0	101
Deep concentration	103
Decision making	104
Conclusion: Living 100% in choice	107
References	111
About the author	119
Other books by Darren Fleming	121
Mindset Mastery programs	123
Additional resources	123

PREFACE

WE'RE PRISONERS OF HABIT: LIFE WITHOUT MINDSET MASTERY

A review of the self-help books in any bookstore could leave you feeling despondent. With very few exceptions, these books are written from a deficit perspective. It's as though you have been born *without* something, didn't have the correct chip installed at birth, or have learned maladaptive behaviours that need to be remedied. The best way to do this, the books explain, is by observing certain people and copying what they did. This will set you free from what is holding you back.

After all, it worked for the author.

These books are mostly about habits, discipline, and different ways of thinking. They give us plans for how we should act in any given situation. They see us as victims of our lifestyle, or someone who is incomplete and needs assistance to be better. We are encouraged to understand *The Power of Habits* so we can build *High Performing Habits*. Or if we want to accelerate our success, we'll develop *The 7 Habits of Highly Effective People*. Then we can develop the habit to *Make your Bed* before we *Take the Stairs* to eventual glory.

Atomic Habits suggests we get a habit tracker app to gamify success, presumably because we won't make it without having fun. *Tiny Habits* suggests we need to remove all friction from our tasks to make our success more likely, lest we trip up on the smallest obstacle.

Some of these books contradict each other. *The Alchemist* suggests we listen to our heart and our dreams will come true. But *Thinking, Fast and Slow* says leave your emotions at home when making decisions. Which is it? And how do we leave our emotions at home?

Robert Greene says we can achieve success by learning the *48 Laws of Power* and *The Art of Seduction*. But *How to Win Friends and Influence People* suggests that being interested rather than powerful is more useful.

If none of this works, we should just develop some *Grit* so we can *Feel the Fear and Do It Anyway*, or simply have *The Courage To Be Disliked*.

As a last resort, if we are still stuck, we should just develop *The Subtle Art of Not Giving a F*ck* about it all and get on with our day.

According to these books, if we develop the right habits, discipline and ways of thinking we will be able to manage that internal drive that causes us to do the things we shouldn't do, or not do the things we should do. Once contained, we should be free from these internal drives.

THE PROBLEM WITH RELYING ON HABITS AND DISCIPLINE

The books mentioned above are obviously popular, well known and impactful. They have helped countless people across the world. So what's the problem with them? There are two that I see.

The first is that they set up progress as a struggle between good and evil. We typically use habits to ensure we do the things we know we should do, but often don't want to. Examples of this are going to the gym, making sales calls, or not saying anything if you can't say anything nice. We then use discipline to ensure we don't develop unhealthy habits around the things we like to do. We need discipline to not have that extra drink or piece of cake or binge too much Netflix.

The second problem is one of maintenance. Once you stop using these techniques to maintain habits and discipline you're usually back to square one. Take the common example of a sales rep who has strong habits around making cold calls every Monday morning. Each week she makes them without fail because that's the habit she has established. Naturally, when she goes on holidays she stops following this habit.

Upon her return to work she has to re-establish old habits, but not all are reintroduced. Disciplines need to be re-established so the habits can be supported and old behaviours can be performed. This takes effort.

It's the same with other habits too. When people go on holidays they stop their habits around fitness, diet and social media use. They then have to work hard to get back to how they were before the holidays.

These books suggest we use willpower, discipline and other mechanisms to oppress an inner force – a drive if you will – to control our behaviour and ensure we *don't do* what we shouldn't, or *do* do what we should. This force is seen as the enemy that needs to be countered, corralled and contained to keep us on the straight and narrow path we have set for ourselves. It's as though their methodology for us to improve involves suppressing part of ourselves.

When we use habits and discipline to suppress the inner force that's stopping us from making the cold calls, driving us to have that piece of cake, or calling us to watch the next episode of our current favourite TV show, we are creating a conflict. It's our willpower and habits that keep the inner force at bay. With this strategy we've set our day up as a struggle to be endured. There's no peace in that.

Nowhere in history has the oppressed ever turned to the oppressor with gratitude for having been forcefully changed. No. They continually fight back. When the oppressor is not watching, the oppressed strike back to regain their freedom. It's the same with this force. If we use habits, discipline or willpower to oppress the inner force that causes us to take action we will always be fighting against it. We have to stick to our habits or be doomed to failure. This takes away choice.

What if you're a sales rep and you *don't want to* make those cold calls on Monday, or you *do* want to have that piece of cake, or you *do* want to watch another episode after bedtime on Tuesday night? What then? Well, you'll have the thought of the calls hanging over your head all week. You'll have to deal with potential guilt (or other emotions) about having the cake, and possibly regret about staying up late and bingeing.

You're also breaking your habits. Once you've done it a few times you're back to square one.

This is another internal struggle you have to deal with. That is no fun.

This strategy means you live in a world where all your options are bad. You either have to follow your 'good' habits and do what you don't feel like doing *or* break the 'good' habits and deal with the fallout.

Perhaps that's why so many people have trouble changing their behaviour, and either give up trying or go in search of yet another book on how to do it.

WHAT ARE WE COUNTERING?

What are we countering when we use habits, discipline or willpower to keep us on track? It has to be something. If we need discipline to make cold calls on Monday there must be a force causing us to *not want to make them*.

If we pay close attention we will notice that we feel an energetic sensation causing us to like or not like something. We don't *feel* like making those sales calls, we *feel* like a piece of cake, or we *feel* like watching one more episode before bed.

If we use habits to get around this sensation, we are using habits to override the message we are receiving from our body. Why would we want to do that? There can be no evolutionary benefit in ignoring a message our body is sending us.

Perhaps the problem is not so much the sensation, but rather our understanding of the purpose of it. As we will see, the purpose of the sensation is not to stop us or keep us doing something. Rather it is to *release* programming within us that makes us conclude we either do or don't like something. When the programming is released we can move on from it and it won't bother us again. As the 19th-century psychoanalyst Carl Jung said, until we make the unconscious conscious it will dictate our life and we will call it fate. When we release the sensation we are making the unconscious conscious. It's what the Stoics meant when they said *The obstacle is the way*. Going through what we don't like is the only way to be free from it.

Unfortunately, most people think releasing means giving into it, or going through it means grinning and bearing it. It's not. As you will see, going through means *experiencing*. And, when done properly, experiencing is a lot quicker, easier and more productive than grinning and bearing. When done as outlined in this book you can be free of the things you don't like in a very short period of time.

WHAT MINDSET MASTERY IS

Mindset Mastery is the ability to maintain metal stability and equanimity, regardless of what is happening. It is the ability to stay focused and calm when external forces are pulling us in different directions while expecting contradictory things. With Mindset Mastery we can deal with what needs to be done despite the ever-changing turmoil of our world.

Mindset Mastery is not about always being happy when things go wrong or always maintaining a positive mental attitude even in the most harsh of situations. Nor is it about suppressing or avoiding what we feel so we become immune to what we don't like. Strategies of that sort simply increase the struggle against the sensations in the body. Mindset Mastery is about understanding how we are triggered by events in our environment, so we can act in a way that we *choose* as opposed to reacting out of *habit*.

Mindset Mastery is achieved by giving 100% close attention to the sensations we experience in our bodies *without reacting to them*. This non-reacting keeps our mindset stable and deactivates our habitual reactions to the sensations so we don't have to experience them again and again.

For the sales rep this means deactivating the sensations that make cold calling a chore. If the calls are no longer a chore they can be done now or later without them hanging over her head all week. Without the sensations we can see a piece of cake and not be tempted by it, or we can have it and not feel guilt. This means we can decide to act or not act, as opposed to reacting to the sensation out of habit. This prevents reactive behaviours and avoids the mess that follows.

This is a very simple process, but that does not mean it is always easy. Ironically, like going to the gym, the harder we find this, the greater the progress we are making in that moment. Finding it hard means we are actively breaking the habit of old:

reacting. When we're finding it hard, we're doing the work of undoing the programming that we've been living by.

This all seems very counterintuitive and around the wrong way. But that is because Mindset Mastery is about letting those sensations happen without reacting to them. When we don't react we don't need to fill our day with habits, discipline or willpower to keep on track with our goals. This is how we do less and achieve more.

> **Mindset Mastery is the ability to maintain metal stability and equanimity, regardless of what is happening.**

A WORD ABOUT THIS BOOK

If you want to know what life is like on the other side of the river, you have to go over and have a look. You can't just sit on your side and assess what life is like without visiting.

It's the same with this book. You can't know how well the technique works just by reading about it; you have to apply it. That's what I want you to do from the very beginning.

Many books in this genre will try to convince you their methodology is sound and true and based on the latest scientific research. Early versions of this manuscript had several chapters convincing you that this method is all right and correct. And it is.

But I'm not sure that it would have convinced you that it works, and it only made the book unnecessarily long. If Mindset Mastery remains an intellectual exercise for you it might be fun, but it won't produce results. You have to experience it to get results and to know that it works.

So I'm going to give you the technique at the end of chapter 1, so you can apply it to your life as you progress through the book. I want you to see how it will operate in your world. Test it, try it, and see if it works for you. If it does, great – keep going. If it doesn't, great – keep looking.

But I know if you implement this as I present, you are bound to be successful.

PART I

HOW WE INTERACT WITH THE WORLD

CHAPTER 1
UNDERSTANDING YOUR PROGRAMMING

David had just spent the night with Nicole, the woman of his dreams. She was smart, sexy and seemed to just get him. He wanted to spend the day in bed with her, and then the rest of his life. But there was a problem: David was married to Caroline, and they had three kids.

David didn't set out to have an affair, it sort of just happened. He'd been married to Caroline for 23 years, but over the last few years they'd grown apart – the marriage had become stale. He longed for the days when they had fun together. He'd even tried suggesting they go back to the old nightclub they used to visit, but the thought of the noise turned them both off.

He wondered how life got this way. He always thought there was no way he would have an affair – he knew the havoc it would wreak on the family. He'd seen it with colleagues and friends over the years. But here he was, faking interstate work trips so he could spend some time with a woman he met a few weeks ago. How did this happen?

When he met Caroline at the age of 25 he couldn't believe how lucky he was. Caroline was truly out of his league. There was something about her, but he couldn't quite pick it. Perhaps it was her long blonde hair, or the air of confidence she had as she walked into a room. He was attracted to her cheeky and irreverent personality, sense of humour and ability to talk to anyone. He'd never had a partner who had so many friends, admirers, who could have anyone she wanted, and she wanted him.

The first few years of their relationship were amazing. Fuelled by alcohol and sex they partied, travelled and followed their desires. They lived a care-free life of spontaneity and crazy decisions, living the stories they would tell for years. After a big trip to Europe they decided they were ready for the happy ever after.

But that all seemed like a long time ago now. All that he could remember of the last few years seemed to be kids' sport, work, attending to their ageing parents, and the constant drudgery of suburban life. He couldn't remember the last time he'd had sex with Caroline or when they had had a good night on the booze together. He longed to have that sort of fun again.

Perhaps that is what made Nicole stand out to him. When he met her at the conference he remembers how struck by her he was – she reminded him of Caroline when they first met. Nicole too had blonde hair, an air of confidence, and a cheeky and irreverent personality. When he spoke to her, something stirred in him, something that he had felt all those years ago, but not for a long time. It made him want to get to know her more. After the drinks at the Gala awards he knew the interest was mutual. Before he knew it they were texting regularly, catching up for a drink, and then they crossed the Rubicon.

Now here he was, staring down the barrel. Did he really want to throw away the last 23 years with Caroline for someone he'd only known for a few weeks? With Emily doing year 12 and retirement on the horizon, did he really want to blow up his family, lose the house and half his retirement savings and start everything again? Had he already done that?

He was torn between two worlds and didn't know what to do. When he thought of Nicole he felt excited, energised and young again. But then his mind instantly flicked to Caroline, their shared history, the love of his family and the plans for retirement. He knew Caroline would be devastated when she eventually found out. He now realised how much he loved her. When he thought of the pain her finding out would cause her it was unbearable. How he regretted his choices. But it was too late now.

So he was left with a decision: should he follow his heart and chase Nicole and become the embodiment of a midlife crisis? Or should he come to his senses and stay with Caroline? All his days seemed to be spent flicking between the two options, riding both the highs and lows of each. It was exhausting and mentally draining. But he couldn't get Nicole out of his head. She was his first and last thought every day. Every time the phone beeped with a text message his heart skipped a beat. They just got each other. He felt happy for the first time in years. Surely this means something?

Spoiler alert: it doesn't.

EQUANIMITY: THE SECRET TO MINDSET MASTERY

Have you ever had the experience of waking up in the morning and for a moment not remembering what's happening in your life? It's calm, peaceful and relaxing as you lie there. Thoughts of any kind are yet to enter your mind, and for the briefest of moments you get to experience the equanimity of your mind at peace. The pure bliss is intoxicating.

Then reality slams in. All the memories, thoughts and feelings that make up your life come flooding back and the peace is gone. You start planning out your day and judging what it will be like. You're looking forward to *this*, but not *that*. You're excited about this opportunity, but annoyed about that chore. You'll be seeing that person which will be good, unless you have to see that other person too in which case it won't be.

Before you know it you're caught up in your life and the equanimity you felt for that brief moment is gone.

The equanimity killer

It's not your thoughts per se that take away your mental peace and equanimity. You have to think to get through the day. Without thoughts you couldn't get out of bed, get the kids to school or manage a large team. Thinking is not the problem.

Nor is it the type of thoughts you think. Despite what most people believe, you are not your thoughts. Sometimes thoughts just happen. You didn't want to have that thought about that person doing that thing, but somehow it popped into your head. It's common for completely random things to just pop into your head – whether you want them to or not.

If you pay close attention, you'll notice that every thought – even random ones – generates an energetic sensation in your body. It's easy to spot the large ones – such as love, fear, anger or pride – but they are there for everything else as well.

It's not these sensations that take your peace and equanimity either.

Rather, your peace and equanimity are taken by how you react to these sensations. As you are constantly thinking you are constantly having these sensations. If your body likes the sensation it will crave more of it. If it doesn't like the sensation it will want to avoid it.

It is the craving to either have more or less of these sensations that takes your peace and equanimity.

UNDERSTANDING AND MASTERING OUR REACTIONS

Our peace and equanimity are taken by the body's constant desire for thoughts on how to experience or avoid sensations. It has spent its whole life believing reacting is the only way to respond to the sensations. The body has developed strong habits around reacting, which drives predictable patterns of behaviour. This constant drive to change what it is feeling to satisfy its cravings and aversions is what takes our equanimity. When we can tame the body to not react to cravings and aversions we are mastering our mindset. We can then encounter the world as it is and we can act from choice instead of reacting from habit.

> Our peace and equanimity are taken by the body's constant desire for thoughts on how to experience or avoid sensations.

The sensory–body feedback loop

At the risk of oversimplifying my psychology degree, the way we interact with the world is a very straightforward process. Everything we encounter goes through the four steps of the sensory–body feedback loop (SBFL) before potentially starting again. The sensations we experience from thoughts are created in the third step and our reaction happens at the fourth. It is only at the final step that the loop can be broken. The first three steps are automated and any attempt to change or stop the loop in these steps is doomed.

The steps in the sensory–body feedback loop are:

1. **Cognising.** For us to become aware of anything in our environment, one of our seven sense organs must first register it. We need to see it, hear it, touch it, taste it, smell it, detect the movement of it or think it. If our sense organs can't detect it we won't know it is there.

    Cognising is an automated process. We cannot stop our senses from operating. Sure, we can close our eyes and not see something, but we are still seeing, it is just the inside of our eyelids that we are looking at. It's the same for sound. A hearing person cannot be in the room with music and not hear it. We cannot think a thought and be unaware of it. It's the same for all senses.

2. **Recognising.** Once the brain has detected a sensory input, it starts interpreting it. This is an automated process and can't be stopped. If you hear someone speaking in your native tongue, you cannot *not* understand it. This is the same for every sense. You cannot see a yellow car and not know it is a yellow car. You cannot touch something hot and not recognise that it is hot.

Once recognition has been processed, the brain automatically evaluates the cognition. Using memories of previous encounters with the same or similar cognitions, it forms an evaluation and determines if and to what level it likes or does not like what it has encountered. Once again this is an automated process we cannot stop, even if we've had years of therapy telling us the way we see a situation can change if we just try hard enough.

3. **Sensation.** As soon as the brain has evaluated the sensory input, it generates a sensation in the body to tell it what it has encountered. Without these sensations the body has no way of knowing what is happening and what is required of it. Without these sensations, systems such as the flight, fight or freeze response wouldn't have evolved. Once again, this is an automated process that no amount of affirmations, journalling or speaking with a therapist will change. It just won't.

4. **Reaction.** This is the first and only point where we can stop the feedback loop. There are three ways the body can react to these sensations.

    If the body likes them it will want to experience them more. Left to its own devices, it will chase these sensations to the point that it develops an addiction to them.

    If it doesn't like the sensations, it will want to avoid them. Once again, if it is left to its own devices it will develop aversions to them to the point where it will do all it can to avoid them.

    The body then sets about identifying ways it can act in the world to satisfy these cravings or aversions. This is done by the mind generating thoughts on how to achieve this. These thoughts then restart the feedback loop and the whole process starts again. It snowballs over time.

The third way to react is to *not* react. Don't judge the sensations as either desirable or undesirable – just experience them for what they are: sensations in the body. When we do this the mind does not create thoughts that restart the feedback loop. When we don't react we are taming the body to stop the cravings or aversions that take our mental peace and equanimity.

When we just experience sensations without reaction we are 100% present to what is happening in our body. The mere act of experiencing them deactivates the programming that caused the sensation. This weakens its hold over us. If we perform this non-reaction a few times, that sensation will no longer be triggered within us.

The refractory period

The time it takes the mind to stop generating thoughts about sensations within the body is called the 'refractory period'. If an event happens and you react it will extend the length of this time.

There is no set timeframe within which the refractory period should resolve itself, but generally speaking, the shorter the better – even for desirable sensations. A mastered mindset can resolve it quickly. A non-mastered mindset could continue the refractory period for days, weeks, months and years. Even decades! Theoretically, once the event has passed, if you are not reacting you won't extend the refractory period. This will enable you to be 100% focused on what you are doing next.

People who experience an event – either desirable or not – who keep generating thoughts about the event once it has passed are extending the refractory period.

When we extend the refractory period beyond the duration of the triggering event we are projecting our imagined reality into the world. This imagined reality is generated from the thoughts the mind generates to help resolve the cravings or aversions. When this happens we have moved from reacting to the event to reacting to our memories and thoughts of the event. This causes untold suffering. The event is over, yet with continual reaction to the sensations we are locked into the SBFL and cannot stop the thoughts that generate more sensations. This drives more cravings and aversions that need to be resolved. This constant extension of the refractory period is what drives very real traumas such as post-traumatic stress disorder (PTSD).

When we do this we are causing ourselves lots of suffering by reacting to the thoughts in our head. If we stop reacting to the sensations in our bodies we will stop the thoughts that drive suffering.

ALL LIFE IS SUFFERING

It was the Buddha who said that all life is suffering. For a chap who was supposed to be enlightened this seems pretty down.

But when you consider the constant struggle we experience chasing cravings and battling aversions, you can see how right he was. It was for this reason that he suggested we should avoid cravings and aversions all together by not reacting – having no judgement. Don't be attached to wanting or not wanting anything. Experience whatever happens for what it is, but don't let it take your equanimity. Be with it 100% and observe the message coming from the body. Then when it's gone, experience the next thing that comes along.

It dawned on him that this was the right thing to do when he realised that everything in the universe is impermanent. Even if you get what you want, it will eventually leave, so don't be attached to it. Thankfully, this is true for aversions too. If you get what you don't want, just experience it knowing that it will eventually pass.

The law of impermanence

Everything in the universe is impermanent and is in a constant state of change. We all grow old and then we die – that's the biggest change we can get. Everything else changes too. The days change, the weather changes, the sun changes, the seasons change, our bodies change, our politics changes, the environment changes, our family changes, what we like changes, what we want changes. Everything changes. Nothing stays the same. The realisation of this was the Buddha's moment of enlightenment.

The Buddha realised that the sensations we experience in our body are also subject to change. They will not last for ever. If we crave certain sensations we will be disappointed if we can't access them, or if we do, when they fade. And if we have an aversion to experiencing some sensations we will be upset when we eventually experience them. All sensations – even undesirable ones – will eventually move on. So why get attached to them and let them take your peace and equanimity?

The term he used to describe this was 'anicca' (ah-nit-cha) – the law of impermanence. Physicists call it the law of entropy. Over time everything moves from order to disorder. To want something to not change is setting yourself up to be unhappy because it *will* change, leaving you with exactly what you don't want. This will take your mental peace.

> **Everything in the universe is impermanent.**

When the Buddha came to realise the impermanent nature of everything in the universe, he realised that if you attach your peace and equanimity to *anything* you are basing your happiness on something that will change. That would then change your happiness. So he hypothesised that cravings and aversions would always lead to unhappiness. The simple act of not creating cravings and aversions would lead to mental inner peace and equanimity. He suggested non-attachment to the sensations in your body and just experiencing them for what they are.

It's pretty hard logic to argue with.

Screw the Buddha – I want stuff!

At first glance, that's a fair attitude to have, but it might be a bit shortsighted. The Buddha didn't say don't work towards goals, nor that we should sit at home all day doing nothing. In fact, the Buddha said you should work very hard and diligently towards what you want to achieve. What he said was we should not attach our equanimity to whether we get it or not. If you want a promotion, develop the skills necessary, apply for the role and go to the interview and give it your best shot. But if you don't get it, don't let that take your equanimity. The decision is made by people other than you, and you cannot control what they do. If you can't control what others do, why base your happiness on their decision?

It's the same for landing that sale or recruiting staff. Do what you need to do achieve the goal, but don't let the decisions of others that you don't control influence your equanimity and mental peace.

Go for what you want, but don't let the outcome determine your happiness.

So ... should you be apathetic?

No.

There is a difference between apathy and non-attachment.

Apathy is when you don't care. Those who express that they don't care often care very deeply but are usually suppressing any sensations related to the situation so they can avoid the suffering of not getting what they want.

Non-attachment means you fully experience any sensations that arise in the moment and observe them as they are. It means completely experiencing them without letting them disturb your peace. Be 100% focused on what you are feeling – either desirable or undesirable – and experiencing it for what it is. Just don't become caught up in it.

Think of non-attachment as acceptance. Acceptance is about engaging with life without having it need to conform to the way you think it should be. You accept others have made a decision that is best for them, even if it generates an undesirable sensation within you. They have the right and agency to do that. Acceptance will allow you to see things as they really are and move on.

Accepting means you don't label the sensations, own them, judge them, fight them, justify or explain them. You just experience them.

Acceptance is what this whole book is about.

Does that mean you need to sit back and let people walk all over you?

Once again, no.

Non-attachment does not mean becoming a doormat and letting others walk all over you. It means not letting the world around you take your equanimity. If you miss out on a promotion, but feel there are legitimate grounds to appeal missing out on the promotion, go for it. Just don't go for it out of anger or spite.

> **Accepting means you don't label the sensations, own them, judge them, fight them, justify or explain them. You just experience them.**

HOW TO BECOME NON-ATTACHED

Being non-attached or non-judgemental about sensations sounds all well and good, but how do you do it? You can't stop thoughts once they've started, so what can be done?

Being non-attached is about being aware of what you are thinking and what is driving it. It's about getting out of your head and into your body.

Below are the *Six Don'ts* of Mindset Mastery you can apply as you read the rest of the book. Every time you come across something that you either agree with, disagree with, think is funny or have some other reaction to, detect what you can sense in your body. When you do detect a sensation, apply the *Six Don'ts*:

- Don't label it (agree, disagree, that's good or bad, and so on).
- Don't own it (this is just how I feel about this sort of content).
- Don't judge it (make it right or wrong).
- Don't fight it (suppress the sensation).
- Don't justify it (I've got a right to feel this way).
- Don't explain it (I feel this way because I read elsewhere …).

Just observe and experience sensations as they exist in your body.

Making the unconscious conscious

The steps above can be difficult. The easiest way to do them is when a thought related to a sensation comes up, ignore the *thought* by placing all your attention on the *sensation*. The thoughts will continue in the background as you do this. Let them continue – don't try to stop them. Just focus on the sensations in your body.

When we apply the *Six Don'ts* we are enabling the unconscious to become conscious. When we experience sensations without reacting we are no longer being driven by the unconscious programming in our body. We are letting it come to the surface where we can become conscious of it. When this happens its influence on our life will be greatly reduced.

There are multiple reasons why this is often harder than it sounds. The main reason is we've spent our whole life training ourselves to do the exact opposite. The rest of the book unpacks what those reasons are and steps you through in detail how to stop the sensory–body feedback loop by not reacting to sensations.

How do I enjoy life without reacting?

Not reacting is not about killing all emotions and maintaining a stony cold disposition lest you trigger the SBFL. That would be a depressing way to live.

Experiencing the sensations in your body means being 100% present to them and the 'message' they are sending you. If the message you are receiving is causing you to smile and express happiness, then do that. If the sensations are causing you to cry and express sadness, then do that. Focusing on the sensations means you don't reactivate the SBFL by generating new thoughts and meanings about the sensations. Experience them without creating stories about them.

HOW THIS AFFECTS US DAY TO DAY

Thinking back to David, it's easy to see how his mental peace and equanimity would have been smashed by his affair. Craving the excitement of his next encounter with Nicole would have been almost unbearable. But this would have been instantly countered by the aversion to what he was doing to Caroline, his family and himself. He would have spent most of every day bouncing between the two. This would have taken up all his mental real estate and been emotionally exhausting. If you've ever been torn between two important and conflicting ideas you know what it's like.

If David had understood the SBFL he could have been in a very different place if he wanted to. When he met Nicole he could have simply experienced and enjoyed the sensations she triggered in his body. If he'd simply experienced them they would have dissipated without him needing to react. Then he would not have craved them more and the relationship would not have progressed based on the sensations.

It's the same for you and me. We may not be dealing with cravings and aversions as big as an affair and blowing up our family, but when we chase certain sensations and not others we experience the same cravings and aversions that drive the SBFL. When we think of the week ahead and see that it's full of kids' sport, work and attending to ageing parents we will experience a sensation from those thoughts. If we react with aversion to the sensations of those parts of our lives and want to avoid them, it drives us to sit on our phone at the kids' sport, daydream while at work and not enjoy the remaining time we have with our ageing parents. We miss our life as it happens in front of us, all because we have attached a craving or aversion to sensations we have experienced in our body.

It's the constant reacting to the cravings and aversions that takes our mental peace and equanimity. When we are caught in this constant feedback loop we have to continually recalibrate our reactions to bodily sensations in an effort to change our thoughts and the eventual sensations we experience. When we are feeling something we have an aversion to we will try to find a craving to replace it with a desirable thought. We will then fight the impermanence of the resulting sensation. This process goes on all day every day, causing us to be constantly vigilant. This is exhausting.

To establish Mindset Mastery so we can do less and achieve more, we need to stop reacting to the sensations in the body. Stopping the way we react to the sensations in our body relies on us understanding how energy drives the mind. That is what the next chapter is about.

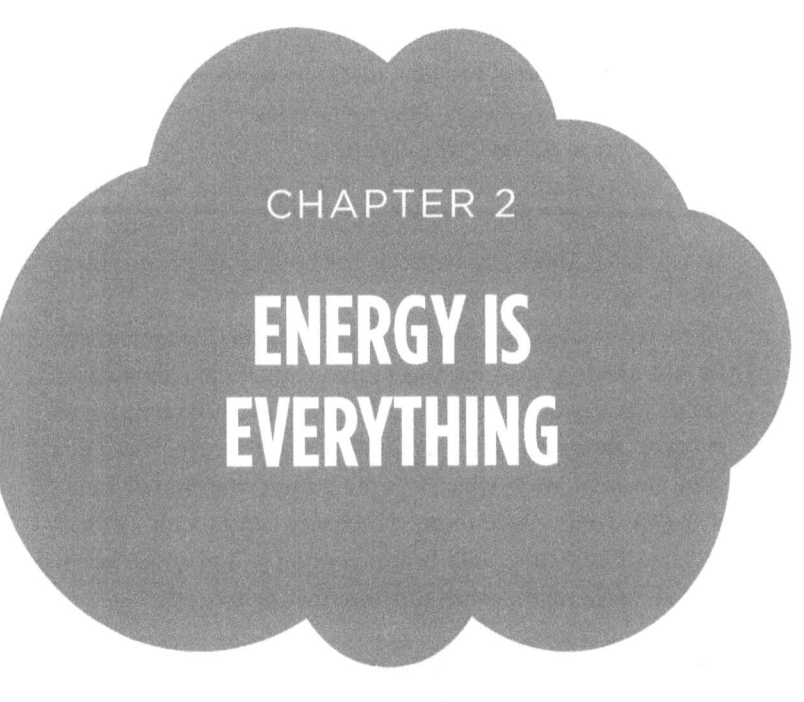

CHAPTER 2

ENERGY IS EVERYTHING

THE ATOMS INSIDE YOU

Over the last 13.8 billion years or so, the atoms that are currently creating what you call your body have had a remarkable journey. Let's consider one of the atoms of hydrogen inside you right now.

To get to be part of you now, that atom was born in a star in a galaxy far far away. At some time over the last 4.5 billion years it made its way to the rock we call Earth.

While on Earth, that atom has been joined to many things, including another atom of hydrogen and an oxygen to form what we call water. This water molecule has been in the oceans, rivers and clouds.

One day it fell to Earth as a raindrop. It hit the ground and was absorbed. A seed that was in that ground then 'drank' it in and used it to grow blades of grass. A cow munched on that grass and took possession of that molecule of water. It then passed that molecule out in milk, which was put into a carton and delivered to the local cafe. Once there, the hipster barista with a fantastic beard frothed the milk before pouring it over some freshly brewed single-origin coffee to create that perfect cafe latte you consumed this morning.

That atom is now part of you. It is currently in a cell keeping you hydrated. Later today the cell will excrete it and it will travel to your bladder and you will pass it out into the toilet. From there it will travel through pipes to the treatment plant and eventually will be pumped into the ocean where it will go on another amazing journey.

It is the same story for every atom in everything you see before you. Each atom of everything has been on its own random journey across the universe through space and time before making its way to be part of your world today.

It has taken 13.8 billion years for the atoms in you and in front of you to be where they are in this moment. It truly is remarkable. Considering the forces and the journey the atoms of you and the things in your world have been on, you can see how little control in life we actually have.

Control – you have none

If the atoms that create the world in front of you have taken billions of years to come together in this order, we can safely say the world doesn't need our input or advice on how things should be. We pretty much have no control or influence over the world around us.

Sure, you might be able to move things from here to there, or even build a house or an office block, but that is minor compared to what has happened to cause the world to be the way it is. In fact, if you were instantly extracted from the world you are in, pretty much nothing would change. We see this on a daily basis. When someone dies, the world goes on without them. Yes, there is a lot of turmoil for the people close to the deceased, but the world goes on and they need to find a new way of operating in it. It will be the same for you and me when we depart.

The universe has spent billions of years making the world just the way it is and has played it out perfectly for us to experience, and yet some people still complain about it. They complain that it is raining, that someone cut them off in traffic or that their cafe latte is too hot, cold, strong, weak or whatever. The universe has created the world to be the exact way that it is now, and they complain about it because they think there is a better way for it to be.

There is a special term for this type of person: whinger. Unfortunately we all fall into this category at some time.

> **There is a special term for this type of person: whinger.**

Whingers

Whingers think they know better than the universe. They can see what the universe has provided in all its glory – from massive galaxies containing billions of stars through to microscopic proteins and molecules that create life – and think that somehow the universe got it all wrong right where they just happen to be! How lucky are we that they are there to help the universe out!

It's a localised problem that the whinger has. They have no problems with how things are on the other side of the universe. They never say a galaxy 100 million light years away should be different. Nor are they too concerned with what is happening across town – they are all fine with that. They are even unconcerned with what is happening in the office down the hall. But when it comes to the room they are in and the way that people are acting around them, they believe they have far more insight into how things should be than the universe does.

The whinger spends their time believing there is a set way things should be for them to be happy. What they fail to realise is that the world in front of them is unfolding according to predictable patterns governed by the laws of physics, biology and chemistry. It has been following these laws for the last 13.8 billion years without error and they have the opportunity to be the only person *ever* to experience their version of it as it unfolds in that very moment. Yet the whinger wants something to change so they can feel better inside.

The problem the whinger has is not really with the way the world is in their immediate vicinity, but rather the energetic sensations they are experiencing from the SBFL as it is activated by the environment. At a point in their life they picked up some programming that caused them to have an aversion to what they are feeling. They now assume it's because of something the universe has caused to happen. Their reaction to the sensation is to demand that the universe change just a little bit so their senses won't encounter what is happening and trigger the feedback loop. This is arrogance on a cosmic level!

Take the case of a teenager not wanting to clean their room after being asked. When they hear their parent ask them to clean their room, the SBFL kicks into gear and they will experience a bodily sensation in relation to the request. If they don't like the resulting sensation they will try to avoid it. Perhaps they will also have a thought about having to put their phone down while they clean. The thought of the phone being out of their hand for even the briefest of moments again activates the SBFL and causes a sensation they don't like. To avoid those sensations they remain lying on their bed staring blankly at their phone.

COMMON BUT UNPRODUCTIVE WAYS OF DEALING WITH SENSATIONS

There are three main ways we deal with the energetic sensations to which we have an aversion. The first is to procrastinate – kick the sensation down the road. Avoid the situation and avoid thinking of it so the sensation is not experienced. This works to avoid the sensation, but it doesn't fix the problem – it just avoids it.

The second is to negotiate. When we use this strategy we seem to be negotiating with the sensation for an outcome that is suitable to us. The teenager might negotiate along the lines of *I'll make my bed then check my phone for a bit before cleaning the floor*. It might sound reasonable to reward yourself with the phone, but it doesn't really make sense. After all, who or what is the teenager negotiating with? It can only be themselves. So negotiation must surely be a sign of madness!

The third strategy is the due-date. For the teenager the due-date is a deadline often imposed by others. Perhaps friends are coming over and the room has to be cleaned before they arrive.

Or perhaps parents won't take them to the party unless the room is clean. When we operate under this strategy we just have to push through the discomfort of the sensation and get the job done.

While these strategies work to avoid the sensations, they are hard work and don't fix the problem. At a later time, not only do you still have to deal with the sensations, but you also have to deal with the problem too.

You may have noticed these strategies in yourself too. We all procrastinate, negotiate with ourselves or eventually stick a due-date on tasks that we have to do at home or work. That's why people lock themselves in their office so they can get that work done before the deadline.

The most productive solution for dealing with the sensations is to just experience them. Focus on what you are feeling and apply the *Six Don'ts*. When you do this, the law of impermanence kicks in and the sensations deactivate themselves. When they deactivate themselves you are making them conscious and they won't direct your life any more. It really is that simple.

WHY WE DON'T FEEL THE ENERGY IN OUR BODY

Feeling the energy in our body is a relatively simple thing to do, once we get back into the practice of doing it. Unfortunately there are a few reasons why we don't do that.

We were not taught how

Sadly our Western society has not taken too well to the idea of getting to know the energetic sensations in our body. We have collectively agreed that it is the logical rational mind that should control what we think and do. For many centuries Western medicine has treated the mind and body as separate and unrelated entities. They simply treated the body with no consideration for the mind and vice-versa. Thankfully this is now changing.

When I went to school in Western Sydney in the mid 1980s we were taught that *any* energetic sensation we had in our body was bad. If we had a desire to move, speak, say something in class we were told that it was the Devil trying to find work for idle minds. We had to suppress what we experienced in our bodies just to make it home alive that day!

But I don't think this is true. I reckon the teacher was just using this as a control mechanism.

The energetic sensations are simply our body responding to what it is experiencing in the environment. Unfortunately the sensations we experience are beyond the language of most people.

> **The energetic sensations are simply our body responding to what it is experiencing in the environment.**

It's too complex for words

The way we label energetic sensations in our body is often lazy and limited.

In *Atlas of the Heart* Brené Brown unpacks one of her studies on emotional vocabulary. Participants were asked to label the emotions they were feeling as they went about their week. The results shocked her. The average participant could identify just three emotions – happy, sad and angry – that they experienced during the week. Sure, they would have experienced more, but they either didn't identify them or mislabelled them. This means they are either not noticing with any great detail what is happening in their body or they are unable to express what they are feeling.

If you can't detect or correctly label what you are feeling, how can you know what is going on?

This could also be a limitation of language. How would you describe love? How would you describe fear?

Perhaps you could describe love as an overpowering welling up of energy within you that rushes from the centre of your body in an upward and outward direction. That sounds fair.

But that could also describe fear, or frustration, or excitement.

We also use the one word to describe many different sensations. I love my wife, my kids, and sailing. The energetic sensations I feel for each of these loves is very different, as is the love and how it would be enacted. Yet in English we only use the one word for all of them.

These energetic sensations evolved very early in our evolutionary past. We used them to communicate before we developed language. As such, they are a completely different communication system to the spoken word. Perhaps this is why some people find them hard to talk about.

A WORD ON LABELLING

The energetic sensations I'm speaking of are often called emotions or feelings. While they can be labelled that, I'm steering clear of those terms here for a few reasons.

The first is that when we put a label on a sensation we introduce a whole world of complication. If you label an energetic sensation you feel when you present to the Board as nervousness, you could introduce a whole lot of unnecessary noise to what you are doing and this is not useful. For example, you might think of the last time you spoke at the leadership off-site and were nervous. You might also think of that time you had to chase away a large spider for your daughter and felt a sense of nervousness and fear. After that, you might get a sense of what it was like the last time you went for a job interview.

As you're about to speak to the Board, bringing in all these stories through the word 'nervousness' is not helpful.

The second reason is that we have no way of knowing if the sensation you label as nervousness is the same as what I label as nervousness. When I stand at the front of the room to speak, the label I could give to the sensation is excitement and fun, whereas you might label it as nervousness.

The final reason for avoiding the terms of feelings and emotions is that there is no set definition of what each of these terms refer to. In *Atlas of the Heart*, Brown states that there are in excess of 70 definitions that are in use for emotions and feelings. If the researchers can't agree on a definition, I think it is well worth steering clear of the terms.

Think back to David and Nicole in chapter 1. When David was with Nicole, he would have experienced some sensations. To say that he was feeling love, lust, desire, excitement, fear, trepidation or anything else would simply be a self-serving story. He was not feeling any of those words. He was feeling a sensation that he labelled as a word that would have suited his motivations at the time.

HABITUATION

Right now, can you feel this book in your hands? Probably. But what about the chair you're sitting on? Before reading that line, were you aware of the sensation of your bum sitting on it? How about the clothes on your skin, the zephyr from the air-conditioner blowing across your face? We can feel some of these sensations all the time (the book in our hands) and not others, like our bum on the seat.

In psychology we use the term 'habituation' to describe the brain's process of filtering out any constant sensation coming from our body. It's why you only hear how loud the fridge is when the compressor *stops* working and its noise is removed from the room. Your brain had habituated to that sound coming through your ears. We feel the book constantly as we are always moving it, but as we are still in the chair we don't recognise it.

While this sounds like a wonderful cognitive function to have – and it is – it becomes a problem when habituation is generalised and we start ignoring other sensations the body is sending us. Unfortunately we do this all the time.

Every sensory experience we encounter is registered in the body as a sensation. It's easy to spot the large ones – the thought of someone you love, or something you fear, or the pride you feel when your child says something insightful. We easily feel that in our body and can identify our reactions to them. But it's not so easy to spot the physical manifestation of the more mundane sensory encounters and how we react to them. What sensations do you experience when you think of what you should have for lunch, or whether or not you should make those sales calls? What sensations do you experience when your ears sense that colleague slurp their coffee again. It has to generate a sensation within you to which you may react. If you can't detect the sensation you won't know how you react to it.

HOW TO OBSERVE SENSATIONS

There is a very simple body scan you can do to observe what you can sense in your body. Simply focus on each part of your body, part by part, and observe what is there. First your scalp. What can you sense? Is there an itching, a sense of temperature, or if you have a shaved head like me, perhaps a slight breeze?

Then your forehead. What is there? Your temples, then your eyes, cheeks, jawline, mouth, ears, nose and back of head. What can you feel in each of these areas?

Continue this down all parts of your body noticing what you can sense. If you can't sense anything, that's fine – perhaps spend a bit of time focusing on it to notice if anything pops up.

The sharper your mind is, the more you will notice. Don't force any sensing – just observe what is either there or not there.

You can increase the sharpness of your mind by repeating this scan daily and by focusing on smaller and smaller parts of the body. Instead of focusing on the whole arm, try the upper arm, elbow, forearm, wrist, hands and fingers. A good amount of time to start with is three to four minutes, but the longer the better. If you can start at 10 minutes that's great.

When you do this, you are also increasing the power of your concentration. Yes, your mind will wander during this scan, and that's okay. Just bring your attention back and continue. When you have noticed that your mind has wandered you're actually present to your thoughts – you are noticing what your thoughts are doing and this is a very good thing.

When you practise this scan regularly you will become more attuned to sensations appearing in your body in response to your environment. This means you will be able to give your attention to them and let them deactivate themselves without creating cravings or aversions.

WHAT TO LOOK FOR

There is no right or wrong sensation to observe. One type of sensation does not mean anything more or less than any other. For ideas on what to pay attention to, familiarise yourself with this list:

- Skin sensations:
    - temperature
    - touch
    - tingling
    - itching
    - twitching.

- Muscle sensations:
    - twitching
    - cramping
    - fatigue
    - recovery.

- External stimuli:
    - shoes on feet
    - clothes on skin
    - limbs resting on something
    - your butt on the seat
    - this book in your hands
    - air blowing on skin.

- Aches and pains:
    - sore back
    - sore neck
    - headache
    - sore joints.

- Digestive:
    - indigestion
    - reflux/heartburn
    - hunger
    - gas.

This list is not exhaustive. Practise doing this body scan daily. It will only take a few minutes and will give you a greater awareness of what is happening in your body.

Best of all, this scan can be done while in a meeting. If you're having a conversation with your team, pay attention to what is happening in the meeting and what is happening in your body. This simple act of paying attention will quieten the voice in your head. If the meeting is challenging or triggering you, paying attention to any sensations will deactivate them.

Observing the SBFL in action

You can use this scan to observe how the SBFL operates in real time. It's simply a matter of putting an extended timeframe on this exercise.

Allocate 15 or more minutes for this exercise. Sit in silence with your eyes closed and perform the body scan. Do not move a muscle for the full 15 minutes. If you're like most people, within a few minutes your body will start to become restless and want to move. It has an aversion to sitting still. But hold strong. You have put aside 15 minutes to do this so stick to it and see how the body reacts.

The body will cause the mind to come up with all types of thoughts as to why you should stop this exercise. It will want you to open your eyes and see what is happening in the room. It will then start activating memories that it hopes you will find important enough to address in that moment so you will stop sitting still. If this doesn't work, it will start throwing all sorts of excuses at you as to why it should move. This could range from creating aches and pains in your body, to manufacturing an emergency that you need to attend to right now. This is nothing more than the body having an aversion to sitting still.

But perhaps the thought of doing this exercise for 15 minutes is not something you would even consider – even if you wanted to. Or perhaps you want to, but you just can't find the time in your busy schedule. That is the body's aversion kicking in right there.

It's the same with cravings. If you want to hold back from something you crave (such as chocolate) the body will constantly direct the mind to come up with reasons to why you should have some. This is a losing battle and even strong habits will eventually fail against this.

WHAT THIS GIVES YOU

The more you can detect the energetic sensations in your body, the less reactive you will be to what you are experiencing at the end of the sensory–body feedback loop. This will strengthen your mindset.

As we'll see later, it's the sensations that activate the voice in your head. If the voice is telling you to not do something, it's because the body has an aversion to the energetic sensation it is experiencing. If it wants you to keep doing something, the body is craving a sensation and wants to get more of it. We have trouble mastering our mindset because it's constantly jumping from craving to aversion. This is what distracts us.

When you can identify these sensations you can start to deactivate them simply by observing them and applying the *Six Don'ts*.

More, you'll be able to see what is driving the voice in your head. As we'll see in the next chapter, that voice is just a reaction to the energy that it feels. It then decides if it likes or dislikes the energy and tells you accordingly.

CHAPTER 3

THE VOICE IN YOUR HEAD

Melissa had been pretty good at her job until the downturn. As a senior rep with an annual budget just shy of $800,000, she usually was pretty close to her monthly targets. Sure she had missed them over the last few months, but so had everyone else across the industry. If the industry has a downturn there isn't much that can be done.

This month and quarter were going to be tight ... again. Off the back of this, Melissa couldn't shake the feeling she was living on borrowed time. Considering the downturn, the poor outlook and that she was getting close to long-service leave, she just had a *feeling*. Nothing was ever said, but she could pick up on it when in the office. She liked to think she had a sixth sense for these things. She'd predicted other people getting the chop over the years, and was usually right. She was starting to wonder if she should look for another job.

It was on the long drive back from the country run when the phone rang. When she looked down and saw that it was Richard, her heart sank. The CEO never called her. Her line of communication to the top was through the National Sales Manager. She got her messages from Shona – GM Sales APAC.

Why would Richard be calling me? she thought. *A call like this on a Friday afternoon can't be good.*

In a flash she had a dozen reasons for the call. Her expenses were late again last month, but she did have the updated forecasts to do. *I'm not paid to work all weekend!*

Perhaps I was a little too passive-aggressive in last month's report. Shit.

Last month's sales weren't great either.

It didn't help that she lost the BHP account. But that wasn't her fault. It was a company decision to keep prices high across the network. *He can't pin that one on me. If he brings it up, I'll let him have it. I'm sick of being used as a scapegoat. There's no way I'm going to be thrown under the bus because of a company decision that I wasn't even party to! That's so unfair.*

She shifted her finger to answer the phone, readying herself for the confrontation. As she hit the button her heart sank.

'Hi Richard,' she said as confidently as she could, feeling her blood pressure rising.

'Hi Melissa,' came back the reply before the awkward pleasantries.

'How can I help you?' Melissa ventured.

'You wouldn't have heard yet, but Shona has just quit. Most unexpected. Joan will be acting in her role until we can find a replacement. We'd like you to step up into the role of National Sales Manager. It will mean a bit more interstate travel, but the pay bump is worth it. We'll be advertising both roles in the new year and we'd expect you to apply. You've been a great team player for the last few years and this is a deserved opportunity. I've been super happy with what you've been doing. Keep it up.'

After a bit more chit-chat, Richard was gone, leaving Melissa hurtling along the highway. She was so glad she had always been a team player, a company woman, willing to take one for the team if it meant helping the bigger picture. It was a great company to work for, and now she had her opportunity to make her mark.

And Richard wasn't as bad as everyone had been saying either. Most of the people in the company didn't like him too much, but at least she understood his bind; he has a job to do and that means upsetting people sometimes.

THAT COMPLETE JERK THAT TRIES TO DERAIL US

Like Melissa, we've all got a voice in our head. The one constantly chattering or screaming away. Perhaps you can hear it reading these words to you.

You may remember it from when it was talking at you while you were trying to read the last page. You know what it's like – you reach the bottom of the page and you can't remember a word of what you read, because you were too busy listening to that voice tell you all about something that happened yesterday, or will happen tomorrow, or something funny it saw on YouTube.

Funnily enough, you were there and experienced it all, but the voice still thinks it has to tell you about it, and how well it went … or didn't go.

Or are you thinking to yourself you don't have a voice in your head and that I must be crazy to even suggest it? Yep – that's the voice I'm referring to.

The technical name for this voice is the default mode network. It's just one of the many ways the mind expresses itself. Sometimes the mind generates visualisations, feelings, tastes and other sensory inputs that we can experience through the SBFL. The collective term that we give to these generated sensory experiences are thoughts. The default mode network is just a series of thoughts. To that end, the voice in our head has no more 'importance' or 'authority' than any other type of thoughts. It's just that most of us are in the habit of noticing it more than the other thoughts.

When we can harness the mind's power it behaves and directs all its thoughts towards achieving what we want. When it is under our control there is nothing we can't do.

But when we don't control it we are unable to harness its power. We then see that voice not as our mind, but as a complete jerk that tries to derail us whenever we want to achieve a goal. If Melissa had listened to her voice she might have not taken the call, or started a confrontation with Richard.

Understanding the mind and how and why it generates thoughts accelerates Mindset Mastery. If we don't understand this, we remain stuck, fighting our mind and wondering why we can't concentrate and have the success and peace we want.

> The voice in our head has no more 'importance' or 'authority' than any other type of thoughts. It's just that most of us are in the habit of noticing it more than the other thoughts.

That voice is not you

If you look at how the voice in Melissa's head jumped around, you'll notice that it was really just saying what it thought Melissa wanted to hear. At one point it was preparing a defence for something she wasn't involved in, the next it was reassuring her that Richard was a great bloke and she was happy to be a team player. You've probably noted your voice doing the same. It often tries to get us to do things we don't want to do.

Have you ever had this situation of sitting on the couch after dinner with your loved ones: you're sitting there watching TV without a concern in the world. The dishes have been done after a great meal and you're enjoying a show. You want for nothing.

A scene unfolds on the show you're watching. The main character goes to the kitchen and gets a bowl of ice-cream and starts eating. At that moment you have the thought, *Gee some ice-cream would be nice*.

Until that moment ice-cream was far from your mind. But now that you've seen it the voice in your head starts a conversation with 'you' about whether you should have some or not. It plays out something like this:

Voice: I want some ice-cream.

You: Better not – I'm trying to lose some weight.

Voice: Yeah, but it's been a tough week. You deserve a treat.

You: Not after going to the gym this morning.

Voice: I want ice-cream. I want ice-cream. I want ice-cream. I want ice-cream. I want ice-cream.

You: No. Be quiet.

This goes on for 20 minutes, and we all know how it ends. You get up and get the ice-cream. And because you're hardcore you put some Milo on it. You go back to the couch and enjoy.

When you've finished, you put the bowl down. Ten seconds later the voice starts again:

Voice: Why did you have that ice-cream? You know you're trying to lose some weight. You're hopeless. You'll never lose that weight you fatty-boom-bah. You have no self-control. You're going to have to do a double session at the gym tomorrow. No wonder you haven't been promoted at work either. You can't even keep your word to yourself, why would anyone want to promote you! And while we're at it, another thing you need to know is ...

Then the voice spends the next hour berating you for doing what it wanted you to do.

That voice in your head is not you. You're the one listening to it. It's just an expression of the undirected mind and what it wants: a problem to solve. This desire for a problem is expressed as a thought. As with all thoughts it activates the SBFL which generates a sensation in your body. You then have the choice whether you react to the sensation or just experience it for what it is.

> **That voice in your head is not you. You're the one listening to it.**

If you react with either a craving or an aversion the SBFL will continue and the voice gets louder, generating more and more sensations for you to react to. But if you don't react, the SBFL will cease in relation to the thought and the sensations will be deactivated.

The problem solver

The mind is an amazing problem-solving tool. From helping our ancestors avoid the sabre tooth tiger, to engineering and flying a plane non-stop from Sydney to London, or helping us figure out a Sudoku, it just wants to solve problems.

When used properly the mind has the ability to access and synthesise amazing amounts of information from any and every source. It will then apply that combined information to a situation at hand and provide an insight into a possible solution. It can deliver us a flash of insight that once heard seems so obvious, but prior to hearing it, no one had been able to arrive at.

Unfortunately, when we constantly react with cravings and aversions, the mind takes these as the problems to solve and we get caught in the SBFL. This amplifies the strength of the cravings and aversions, which in turn keeps the loop going.

Thoughts just happen

If we look closely at our thoughts, we will see there is nothing doing the thinking we experience – thoughts just happen. In his 2014 book *Truth vs Falsehood* David Hawkins maps out how thoughts just arise from a primordial soup somewhere between consciousness itself and our awareness of it. Unless consciously directed, they arise in a continual random process, sometimes completely unrelated to the thought preceding or following. We see this when those we are speaking with, mid conversation, ask us a completely random question and expect us to know what they are talking about. The thought had popped into their head and they shared it, as they had with every other thought they encountered while talking to you.

When thoughts are left to their own wandering ways there is nothing to be gained from watching them. Thoughts just pop into our head, exist for a period of time and then disappear again.

The mind believes itself to be a rational actor. It believes its thoughts are based on logic and make perfect sense to anyone experiencing the same situation. This belief is often expressed when people complain with the phrase, 'Common sense is not all that common'. What they really mean when they say this is, 'Why don't you see the world the same way I do?'

THOUGHTS FROM SENSATIONS

When the body reacts with either a craving or aversion the mind creates a thought about what that sensation 'means'. It wants to know how to react so the body can either get more or less of the sensation. Believing itself to be logical and rational, the mind scans the environment to identify what triggered the sensory–body feedback loop, erroneously believing that it caused the sensation.

Once it has identified what it thinks caused the sensation, the mind activates thoughts about how to resolve it. Some of these thoughts are in the form of the voice. When some people express this voice, they often earn the label of whinger. We've all experienced them!

The whinger sets about trying to adjust the world to either attract or repel the sensory objects it thinks is causing the sensations. It blames others for the sensations ('you offended me') and wants them to take action to stop them ('I want you to apologise'), believing that this will deactivate the sensations.

Little does it 'know' that the sensations are originating inside the body at the end of the feedback loop, not in the environment. The body has developed such strong habits around reacting with cravings and aversions that it does not realise there is another way. This means it's only remedy for things it does not like is to blame events external to itself.

The SBFL is so central to the way we process the world around us that we often don't realise we are in the grips of its loops. We become so caught up believing the voice in our head is 'us' ('I've been thinking … ') and think we need to react with either a craving or aversion to what it is saying ('my thoughts are telling me I should … '). Stopping this cycle is a matter of knowing that the voice is just another sensory input at the top of the SBFL (like sight, sound, taste, etc.) and not reacting to the sensation it generates.

SPOTTING WHEN YOU ARE IN THE GRIP OF THE VOICE

There are several ways to spot that you are in the grip of the voice.

A good place to start is realising that unless you're concentrating or have done a good deal of work to understand how you react to the sensations in your body, you are spending most of your day in its grip. This is close to 99.9% of society. Unless you're aware of the SBFL you will be reacting to the sensations the thoughts generate.

In addition to this, there are other observable signs that you are in the grip of the voice.

I'm right, you're wrong

One thing the mind loves more than a craving or aversion problem to solve is its own opinion, in the belief that it is right and others are wrong. After all, what better craving could there be than to always feel right?

For the mind, the thought of being wrong creates a sensation that the body will have an aversion to. It's rare that it will voluntarily do this. This is part of the reason that people can hold so strongly to the notion that they are right and others are wrong even in the face of evidence to the contrary. They simply have an aversion to the sensation of being wrong. Being right feels good and as such the body develops a craving for it.

This is what happens when cravings and aversions are allowed to build and we develop addictions to them.

> **For the mind, the thought of being wrong creates a sensation that the body will have an aversion to.**

Time travelling

The mind loves time travel. It is constantly reliving the past or fantasising and catastrophising about the future. Wins and gains can be amplified so the desirable experiences are remembered as even more desirable. Or, if the past event involved a loss, it will mentally replay the situation over and over again so it can correct what it thinks happened. As a result of this rewriting of history it can either win or be the unlucky victim at the mercy of some other person who thwarted their ability to succeed. Either way, it wins.

Often, undesirable sensations are relived as part of the process of dealing with memories. This is the making conscious of the unconscious so it doesn't dictate our life. Reliving undesirable sensations in this way can help deal with associated memories if you don't react to the sensations.

Chasing sensations it craves, the mind often travels into the future to pre-live how it wants life to play out. It will fantasise about how it will handle situations, how others will react to what you do and say, and how others will then see that it was right all along and they will then agree with what you have put forward. This makes it right and generates a desirable sensation.

Even travelling to the future to pre-live how things will go wrong is an exercise in proving itself right. It plays out what it thinks will happen and comes to the conclusion that it knows how things will go, hence proving itself right.

Through the act of time travel, the mind can solve craving and aversion problems it is creating itself. If it's bored, it can fantasise about the past or future and generate the sensations it wants to experience.

TALKING TO ITSELF

Have you ever noticed that when thinking to yourself about what you should do it is the same voice taking both sides of the debate? If you are debating whether you should have some ice-cream, the conversation from above is more accurately represented like this:

Voice: I want some ice-cream.

Voice: Better not – I'm trying to lose some weight.

Voice: Yeah, but it's been a tough week. You deserve a treat.

Voice: Yeah but if I do it will negate my efforts at the gym earlier today. I won't have any.

Voice: I want ice-cream. I want ice-cream. I want ice-cream. I want ice-cream. I want ice-cream.

Voice: No. Be quiet.

It is the same voice on both sides, pretending it is being impartial. It's not. There is no demarcation as to what side of the debate is 'you'. Are you the first or second 'speaker'? Are there rules for what side 'you' are assigned to? Any identification of you being on one side or the other is simply a reflection of how much you have bought into the idea that the voice in your head is you. The mind is simply using the voice to create an opportunity to generate sensations the body wishes to experience.

If the mind is not being directed, it will set about generating thoughts that will produce sensations the body craves.

> **Any identification of you being on one side or the other is simply a reflection of how much you have bought into the idea that the voice in your head is you.**

HOW TO DEACTIVATE UNWANTED THOUGHTS

You can deactivate unwanted thoughts by observing without judgement the energetic sensations they generate within your body. Apply the *Six Don'ts*, and focus on the sensations in your body. If the mind is generating stories about the sensations, just let it and focus only on the sensations. You have to stop the sensory–body feedback loop. Focus on the sensations and they will deactivate themselves. This is the law of impermanence. This is how you accept that the obstacle is the way. This is making the unconscious conscious. This gives you a mastered mindset.

If you become caught up in the sensations you will generate cravings and aversions for them. This will cause the mind to create more thoughts to satisfy the cravings and aversions. These thoughts are stories you then have to deal with. That's what the next chapter is about.

CHAPTER 4

IT'S ALL A STORY

The flight from Canberra to Sydney usually only takes 75 minutes, but this was no ordinary flight. It was the second attempt to make the journey. The first had to be aborted 30 minutes after take-off. The storms along the flight path were so severe that all airports in Sydney were closed and we had nowhere to land. Going back was the only option.

Now having left at 9:30 pm our small plane was again flying between the clouds. The lightning lit up the night sky briefly before the darkness slammed in again. Lightning bolt after lightning bolt lit up the cockpit as the pilot studied the instruments. The plane shook constantly – enough to make even seasoned travellers like me nervous.

A lot of people don't like flying in small aircraft. Perhaps it's because there's no inflight service or toilet, or the perceived safety in numbers you get on a commercial airline. Or perhaps it's because you can see what the pilot is doing or, often, not doing. They are not always holding the yoke. They rarely look out the window either.

I looked at the pilot through the dimly lit cabin. I could see he had it under control. He was calmly doing his job without a worry for the turbulence outside. He kept his eyes on the instruments, occasionally looked out the window at the lightning, before returning his attention to the panel. He was calm, he was cool and he looked like he was comfortable. He wasn't really doing a lot – just gently holding the yoke to get a feel for the plane as he sat there watching the night go by.

I realised the pilot had it all under control and there wasn't much I could do, even though I was sitting next to him. Not being a pilot – not many eight-year-olds are – I decided to curl up and go to sleep. I knew we'd be safe – my Dad was the best pilot in the world.

An hour later I was woken as the plane touched down at Bankstown airport in Sydney. We went home and I went to bed. To me, that was just another day out flying with Dad. I was so glad he had to do the trip on a Sunday and that I could go with him. It was fun and it was exciting seeing the lightning, and I knew that no one at school would have a story that cool on Monday morning.

Twenty years later I was speaking to Dad about that flight. We talked about how bumpy it was, and I mentioned how exciting it was. He was surprised I remembered it, and I was surprised that he did too. Then he said something that nearly floored me, 'Of course I remember it. That was the most terrifying night of flying I'd had in 35 years as a professional pilot!'

THE WORLD IS AN INKBLOT

In 1918 Swiss psychoanalyst Herman Rorschach developed a unique set of tests to help understand a patient's personality. He showed them a series of carefully designed and printed inkblots and asked them what they saw in them. Rorschach hypothesised that what the patient saw would give an insight into what was in their mind. This could then be used to diagnose schizophrenia and other mental disorders.

While the usefulness as a diagnostic tool has been entirely discounted, what Rorschach had developed was one of the first projective tests. Projective tests allow participants to project what is in their mind onto the neutral stimuli in front of them. They then use what is in their mind to explain the picture.

The power of the inkblot test is that the image has no inherent meaning. There is nothing in the image to suggest anything. This means everyone sees the same neutral stimuli and comes up with a different story. Any difference in any stories between patients has to be from within their thinking.

It is the same with the world we see. What we are looking at has no inherent meaning. A bright sunny day is not always a good day. To a farmer who needs rain, it is terrible. To the bride who is getting married, it is perfect.

Sitting in the plane flying back from Canberra, Dad and I projected different meanings onto the situation. I projected a meaning of an exciting day with Dad at his work. He projected the possibility of danger and what could go wrong.

THE MEANING WE PROJECT

The meaning we project can only be based on the programming inside us. After all, you can't project something you don't have. We call these projections 'stories' and we believe them to be true.

The stories we tell ourselves are directed by how we react to the energetic sensations we experience. If we have a craving for the sensation we will tell ourselves a story that enables us to experience the sensation again. If we have an aversion to the sensation we tell ourselves a story as to why we should avoid the situation in the future.

But if two people can look at the same situation and come up with different stories, whose projection has the most accurate meaning? Should my story be discounted in favour of your story? If so, what criteria should be used to assess it? What happens if the two people then agree on a story and a third person comes along and has their own story? What should happen then? Should they have to change because they came to the party late, or should the debate be reopened?

Perhaps if several people can each see their own story in a situation, the only reasonable conclusion to draw is that, like inkblots, the situation has no inherent meaning. Any story you are seeing in the world is simply a projection of the cravings and aversions inside you.

To put this another way, you're making it all up.

When you say something is good, you are making that up. If you say something is bad, that too is made up.

> **Any story you are seeing in the world is simply a projection of the cravings and aversions inside you.**

Let's take the example of a large sale being missed. You had wanted to land that sale as it would have covered 50% of your monthly budget for the next six months. To tell yourself a story that it is a bad thing you missed the sale is only true for you – not the competition, or for the customer who chose them.

The fact that you didn't get the sale is objectively true, but the story you create around it is not. If you carry a story of *I'm not good enough*, or *the customer is stupid for not choosing me*, or *I am being thwarted by management because they aren't giving me the support I need to win new business*, any decision made on these stories can only end badly. They are not based on anything other than what you have made up.

THE VALUE OF OUR MADE-UP STORIES

Even though the stories we tell ourselves are all made up, they still serve a purpose. In her book *Peak Mind*, neuroscientist Amish Jha explains that one of the innumerable benefits of stories is to transport us to a place where we can road test our ideas. We can rehearse meetings we will attend, try out conversations we will have, and pre-live events we will attend so we know what could happen. In our personal world this is essential so we can manage our relationships and act in a socially acceptable manner. In the corporate world it's useful to ensure we don't waste anyone's time. After all, we don't want to get a chance to finally pitch to that client only to go in unrehearsed!

The problem is we develop cravings for life to unfold in a way that fits our made-up stories. We fall into the trap of believing that just because we have thought a certain outcome should occur, that is what *will* occur. And if it doesn't, we get upset. If we plan to ask the Board for funding for a project and they say no, we get annoyed. But being annoyed was predicated on our craving for our made-up story that the Board would give us funding. So, we are upset because the decision the Board made did not match what we wanted to happen in our made-up story.

That's great in theory, but I've got to make budget

The obvious question on reading this is, 'How do you get anything done if you can't have attachment to the outcome?'

That's a fair question. You must learn to understand the difference between commitment and non-attachment.

Commitment and non-attachment

It can be easier to think about commitment and non-attachment in terms of *what I do vs how I react*.

With commitment, I am committed to doing what I can and should to get the outcome I want. If I'm trying to land a customer I will research their needs, develop a pitch and do my best when I go in. I am concerned about what I do, how I do it and how this will help the customer achieve their goals.

Being non-attached to the outcome is knowing that when the customer makes their decision it will activate the sensory–body feedback loop and I will experience a sensation. Non-attachment means watching that sensation as it rises and exists for a period of time before it fades away, *without* generating more thoughts in the form of stories about it.

Mindset Mastery is not about not trying, not doing the work or not doing anything else we are required to do in our day-to-day life. It is about not craving one outcome over an aversion to another. Set the goal and work towards it. If it comes off – great! Feel the sensations as they arise and experience them before they pass away. Just don't let them take your calm peace and the equanimity of your mind. If the sensations cause you to want to express happiness and joy, do that in the way that you see fit. Just don't react by creating stories about it. Then, start fulfilling the order from a position of peace and happiness.

But if it doesn't come off, that's okay too. Feel the sensations as they arise and pass away, just don't let them take your calm, peace and the equanimity of your mind. If they cause you to feel frustration and annoyance, feel that and express it as you see fit. Just don't react by creating stories about it. Then, pick the next potential customer and start working on landing them from a position of peace and equanimity.

Now I can hear you saying, *Great Darren, but that attitude ain't gonna wash if I miss that big sale!*

Perhaps.

But what are you expecting any other reaction to achieve? If you have put in your best effort and did everything 'correctly' and the sale did not come off, what will reacting to the sensations in your body achieve? Losing your mental peace and equanimity by creating a story about what happened won't help you learn the lessons on offer so they can be applied next time. Nor will it help you land the next client.

Non-attachment does not mean apathy. It means not letting what happens to you take your mastered mindset.

It's easy to have Mindset Mastery when everything is going well. It's your ability to maintain your equanimity and happiness when things don't go the way you want that is the true measure of mastery.

SENSATIONS AND STORIES

As outlined in chapter 3, the mind believes itself to be a rational actor that operates from a position of logic. When the body experiences a sensation the mind reacts to identify the cause of the sensation in the environment and responds to the craving or aversion.

To the mind it's easy to identify what must be done to resolve the situation. That person should go away, another person should come over, specific events should happen the way that it decides and other parts of the environment should act in a way that does not upset it. These are the whingers we all know. You don't have to be a complete whinger to be guilty of this though. If you've ever wanted something in the world to change so it is the way you would like it to be, you are whinging, perhaps in a more socially acceptable manner.

When examined, the whinger has a number of storylines to shape how the world must be so it can resolve the cravings and aversions.

> When the body experiences a sensation the mind reacts to identify the cause of the sensation in the environment and responds to the craving or aversion.

Storylines the whinger uses

The body has become habitualised into a binary response in how it resolves cravings and aversions. Because of this it has developed a number of storylines that can be deployed to give advice on how the universe should change so the sensations are resolved. If ever we are whinging, we are probably using these storylines.

In his 2014 book *Truth vs Falsehood* Dr David Hawkins briefly listed a number of storylines the mind uses to guide itself through situations where it wants the environment to change. Unfortunately, Hawkins never elaborated on the list. Below are those dot points and my expansion of how these storylines play out when the whinger is in full flight:

1. **Phenomena are either right or wrong, just or unjust, good or bad, fair or unfair.** To resolve cravings and aversions more quickly, the mind generates conclusions about parts of the environment based on binary options. These conclusions are general and broad-based. The speed with which it does this seems impressive and enables it to move onto resolving the next sensation without any fuss. Unfortunately this storyline often involves jumping to conclusions.

2. **The 'bad' deserve to be punished and the 'good' rewarded.** Because our reactions to sensations are binary, the mind applies this framework to the cause of sensations with itself as the sole arbiter of what is good or bad. Those opposing its position are classified as bad and need to be punished and taught a lesson. Those who agree with it should be rewarded for doing so. What the storyline fails to accommodate is that good or bad is just a conclusion based on the body's reaction to the sensations at the end of the sensory–body feedback loop.

3. **Things happen by accident or are someone else's fault.** Believing the cause of sensations lies outside the body, the mind does not consider that it could be creating what it is experiencing. Therefore if it is experiencing a sensation, someone must have caused it or it has happened by accident. The major benefit of this structure is it can abdicate all responsibility for how it feels and how it reacts.

4. **It is possible to recognise truth from falsehood.** When the mind detects the body's reaction to a sensation it believes that

the reaction is 'right' for the situation. It therefore assumes that any thoughts it generates in response to the reaction are also right. These made-up stories generate sensations that 'feel right' so it in turn believes that it is. This feeling 'right' is not a reading of being correct, but rather one of familiarity. The body just happens to be familiar with these sensations and assumes they are right. It is confusing the experience of familiar with absolute knowledge of being right. Neither the mind or body has any way of knowing for certain if something is true or not. That is why there will always be charlatans, con artists and politicians who can fool us. It is why those who follow conspiracy theories hold their beliefs with such conviction – they truly believe they are the ones who know.

5. **The world causes and determines one's experiences.** The mind believes the world causes what the body experiences. This is why whingers want the world to be a certain way; they believe *their* way of reacting to situations is the *only* way to react to situations. The mind finds it very difficult to come to terms with the fact the outside world is neutral. If it did come to terms with this, it would mean that it is responsible for the position it finds itself in and has complete control to change it. This could mean change, which could generate unfamiliar sensations which it has an aversion to.

6. **Life is unfair because the innocent suffer while the wicked go unpunished.** This storyline allows the mind to take up the righteous fight to resolve sensations. Once again, this storyline overlooks the idea that what is considered suffering and wicked is merely a result of cravings and aversions.

7. **People can be different than what they are.** The mind believes it has the right to direct how others act so they

don't trigger sensations within its body. This will enable it to experience sensations – and therefore the world – as its body wants. 'If only you'd be more like this and less like that everything would be fine!', is a common refrain in many relationship counselling sessions. What they are really saying is, 'If only you'd be more like this I will experience more/less of this sensation.'

8. **It is critical and necessary to be right.** This sits at the basis of all arguments. This storyline is about ensuring that a particular sensation is not experienced. If the mind admits it is wrong in one instance it could be wrong in other situations as well and this would generate more undesirable sensations. To avoid this, the mind doubles down on ways to avoid the undesirable sensation by trying to win the argument. Therefore winning the argument is not about winning per se, but avoiding an undesirable sensation.

9. **It is critical and necessary to win.** Often the body experiences an aversion to coming second. If it is second, someone could have power over it and inflict more undesirable sensations. This plays out in conversations, arguments and relationships all the time. Perhaps this is why most cultures on the planet have some form of sport.

10. **Wrongs must be righted.** If the body experiences an undesirable sensation in response to something it sees, it uses this storyline to decide that what has happened is wrong and must be righted so it can resolve the sensation. But, once again, what is 'right' or 'wrong' is based on the sensation it experiences and is therefore unique to it.

11. **Perception represents reality.** By definition we can only perceive what our senses send to our brain. These senses activate the SBFL which creates a sensation that the body

reacts to. The mind then makes assumptions and generates more thoughts about the reality of a situation based upon these reactions. As the mind has generated the thoughts and the body is 'agreeing' with them, it believes that the thoughts are 'right' and this represents reality.

If you look closely – and honestly – you will see that at times you will have operated from these storylines. You believe these stories because they feel 'right', 'correct' and 'true', and you wonder why others can't see it that way. The only reason you think they are true is because that is what the sensation from your body is telling you. It may even have led you to assume that it was others – and not you – being unreasonable.

But others also have these storylines about the sensations they experience. They then come to the conclusion that it is *you* who is being unreasonable, and from there arguments begin. When two people use storylines based on their own perspective, an argument is bound to start. Stopping these arguments is as simple as not reacting to the sensations in your body. Just experience them and let them dissipate.

HOW THIS PLAYS OUT

You're sitting in a meeting room with two colleagues discussing how a project should get back on track. Part way through the meeting Andrew gives a less than pleasant description of the people who have repeatedly missed deadlines and have caused the project to fall behind *(the 'bad' deserve to be punished)*. This comment doesn't worry you and you forget about it. Jane, on the other hand, is offended by what is said *(phenomena are either right or wrong, just or unjust, good or bad, fair or unfair)*.

After the meeting, you don't give another thought to what Andrew said, but for Jane, feeling offended *(the world causes and determines one's experiences*), it plays on her mind for the rest of the day and overnight. It continues the next day. She replays the comments over and over and comes to 'realise' that she knows what Andrew really meant by those words (*it is possible to recognise truth from falsehood*). Andrew shouldn't be allowed to say things like that because they offend people (*the world causes and determines one's experiences*). It's not right and it needs to be addressed (*wrongs must be righted*)!

Jane approaches Human Resources and lodges a complaint. It's not that she wants vengeance, but Andrew shouldn't be allowed to say things like that and get away with it. Andrew is called in to HR to explain why he said what he did. Andrew can't understand why Jane is offended and thinks HR are blowing it out of all proportion: people say so much worse than that all the time in the sales department – they are the ones who should be investigated! (*life is unfair because the innocent suffer while the wicked go unpunished*); he can't see what all the fuss is about and doesn't understand why he is being asked to apologise. This is political correctness gone too far (*perception represents reality*)!

To decide what should be implemented to assist Andrew through this, HR retire to consider the options. The case manager in the HR team is that chap who thinks that *people can be different than what they are*. As the keepers of the policies and guidelines on how things should be done he sees it as his duty to ensure that this behaviour is stamped out. Andrew is then sent on a two-day course so he isn't like that again in the future (*phenomena are either right or wrong, just or unjust, good or bad, fair or unfair*).

The following Monday Andrew returns to the office, and when contacted by HR to see how the course went he gives enthusiastic lip-service to what he has learned and vows to be better in the future. Of course he doesn't believe any of it, because *it is necessary and critical to be right* so there is no way he is going to back down. But to get HR off his case, he'll say what he has to. Over the last few weeks he has developed an aversion to dealing with them.

Through the recent experience he can see what is really going on – he is the only one who can *recognise truth from falsehood*. He can see this now and it's just not worth the hassle of it all.

Of course Jane has her own version of this. As does HR. As do you. As do I.

Anywhere people are involved, if the mind is not controlled, the voice will adopt the most useful storyline to explain why it is right and everyone else is wrong. It will do this along the lines of its cravings and aversions.

This happens in every organisation, community group, family setting, social environment and any area where people come together. This is just what happens when we don't realise that all the stories we tell ourselves are simply made up.

* * *

As we flew from Canberra to Sydney that night, both Dad and I projected different stories onto the inkblot that was our world. I projected one of safety and eventual boredom that was so strong I went to sleep. Dad projected one of potential danger. Who was right? As we made it back safely perhaps I was. But as Dad was fond of saying, 'An experienced pilot uses their years of training and experience to avoid situations where they need to use their years of training and experience.' So perhaps he was.

PART II
MINDSET MASTERY IN ACTION

CHAPTER 5
THE POWER OF DOING NOTHING

I remember the exact moment I decided I would date Ali. It was 3:36 pm on Friday 26 May 2017. I was in Melbourne at a Thought Leaders Business School immersion. This business school was for people who made their living selling what they know in book format, training programs and keynote speeches. We all run practices by ourselves and most don't have any local support staff. We'd get together every 90 days for professional development and to plan out the next quarter.

At 3:36 Lisa and Colin took to the stage and announced the first ever Thought Leaders Ball. It was to be held as a Christmas party at the Eureka Tower – the tallest building in Australia – overlooking Melbourne.

And the best part? We were encouraged to bring our partner.

At that exact moment I knew my amazing partner would love it. This would be an opportunity to see that we really could inhabit each other's worlds and that she would like my friends and they would like her.

The only problem was, I was single. I'd been so for about seven years. Sure I'd had girlfriends but nothing serious. Lots of lovely people, but not the connection that was needed for marriage.

But in that moment I knew I would have someone. I felt more confident than anything in my life that it would happen – I would have an amazing partner to bring along. She would be so amazing that she would be worth marrying. At this stage I had never met Ali.

I looked at my diary to work out when I was going to meet her. My diary was chockfull of travel from June to end of August. So I closed off September. After all, if you meet a lovely lady you have to be in town to get to know her.

At the end of July, a lady I was seeing decided she didn't want to see me anymore because she could see there was no long-term future for us. The following morning I received a call from another friend to attend a singles event that night. At the event I met a lovely lady by the name of Ali and we swapped numbers.

But I didn't call her. I knew I was travelling every single week through August, and the weekends when I was at home I had my kids so we couldn't meet up.

At the end of August I sent her a message asking if she remembered me and letting her know I'd be at a singles event the coming Friday. To my surprise – and excitement – she instantly sent back a message saying she was already booked in for that event and she'd see me there.

We danced and karaoke'd the night away and within a few weeks I knew she was a perfect fit and would love the Ball. At the Ball she slotted right in as though she had known everyone for years. She loved my friends and they loved her.

Three years later we married and now have the most amazing life imaginable.

DOING NOTHING

When Lisa and Colin announced the Ball, I remember having the thought of, *Yep. I'll have someone who will fit right in*. I felt an energetic sensation in my body. It was a kind of buzzing and it just sat there.

Normally I'd label a sensation like this as excitement, anticipation or something similar, and become caught up in the intoxication of it. But I didn't. I just watched what was happening. I was 100% present to what was occurring in my body and how I was being triggered by my environment. I watched the energy as it moved through my body. The sensation did what it wanted to do and eventually it subsided.

I remember being calm and certain about what was required for what I needed to do. I knew I would have to close my diary for September – and forgo any income as 95% of my income came from interstate work. Not reacting to the sensations I was experiencing when I thought of Ali made it easy to not contact her during August. After all, there is no point in contacting an amazing lady only to say *I'll see you next month!*

When you can simply observe and experience, but not react and become caught up in the sensations happening from the sensory–body feedback loop, you are at the point of Mindset Mastery. When you are at this point, you are 100% in the moment, experiencing life as it is without the mind creating stories from the cravings and aversions you are experiencing.

In that moment, I'd managed to stop reacting to the sensations in my body and just knew I would achieve the outcome I wanted. I didn't know how, but I knew it would happen. It turns out that breaking the loop is as simple as doing nothing and just observing the sensations in your body. That's it.

When we break the loop we drop all preconceived ideas about what's happening. We see the world in front of us as it is, unencumbered by stories, programming and more thoughts triggered by our reactions. When we do this, we let the law of impermanence deactivate the sensations and this makes the unconscious conscious. When we stop reacting and do nothing and experience the sensations we are letting the obstacle be the way. We can see the world as the inkblot that it is, a neutral event that we had previously applied a story to.

When we do nothing and the sensations dissipate, we are often met with a sudden burst of happiness, laughter and love. As more and more sensations are released through continual non-reacting, life energies of peace, love and joy start to emerge. When we stop reacting we can see the reality of what is in front of us without stories clouding our perception. We can often see the futility and small mindedness of what we were holding on to. We now see the events in the outside world as having no intrinsic meaning. We end up laughing at how we allowed ourselves to get caught up in our cravings and aversions and the stories we created around them.

When we break the loop we are doing nothing. We are not being distracted by events, the voice in our head or desires we have for any given situation. This is a mastered mindset.

The process of deactivating is incredibly simple – we literally do nothing and just experience the sensations. But this simplicity is in stark contrast to what we have been taught to do. It is also in contradiction to what the body is addicted to doing: reacting and generating more thoughts that trigger the SBFL. Because of this, doing nothing is not always easy.

> When we break the loop we drop all preconceived ideas about what's happening. We see the world in front of us as it is, unencumbered by stories, programming and more thoughts triggered by our reactions.

To explain what doing nothing is, it's helpful to understand what doing nothing is *not*. When we know this we will know what not to do. When we stop doing this we will be doing nothing.

THE FOUR WAYS WE DON'T DO NOTHING

There are three primary ways we 'do things' to manage aversions and one we use to manage cravings. Below I outline how we often use these strategies for a common but uncomfortable workplace situation: giving a presentation.

Avoid

Avoidance is where we take actions to avoid people, places and things that trigger the sensory–body feedback loop and the sensations we don't want to experience. This is very common for public speaking and presenting. It is also common in areas of conflict within the home or workplace. 'I just don't want to talk about it' might avoid the sensation in the moment, but not the problem long term.

Ways we avoid triggering the SBFL in relation to public speaking may include not applying for jobs that require us to speak, keeping a low profile so we aren't asked for our opinion, and simply keeping quiet in a meeting. If we are asked to give a presentation we might look to delegate it to one of our team as a 'development opportunity' just to avoid the sensations.

Avoidance takes place in many ways in all areas of life. It's also known as escapism. Nir Eyal in his book *Indistractable* highlights that we use distraction to avoid the pain of life. When we go shopping, to the movies, to the gym, to our lover's place or anywhere else that helps us avoid an unpleasant sensation we are using this strategy.

Indulgence in alcohol, licit and illicit drugs, excessive consumption of TV, excessive sex, pornography or burying ourselves deep in work are common too. In her book *Braving the Wilderness* Brené Brown explains that those alive today are the most numbed, indebted, overworked and tuned-out cohort in human history. Never have we had so many ways of avoiding undesirable sensations as we do today.

Avoiding can also be less sinister and even socially acceptable. In his book *The Inner Self* Hugh Mackay outlines 20 of the most common ways we avoid dealing with the sensations we experience. These include nostalgia, ambition, arrogance, busyness, fatalism and many more. Mackay is quick to point out that we are not always avoiding when we are partaking in these activities, but when we do them to excess, or use them as guidance to what we should do next, they will stop us from getting in touch with our inner self.

Suppress

When we suppress, we feel the fear and do it anyway. We know we don't like presenting, but it's part of the job and we just have to push through that undesirable sensation and get it done. We smother the sensations and pretend they just don't exist. But they do.

The SBFL will always generate a sensation for us to experience. If the sensations are not discharged they will come back in some other form such as irritability, mood swings, tension in the neck, cramps, indigestion, insomnia and many other ways.

Not only that, but when we next have to present, if we have not experienced the sensation and let it dissipate, it will be there for us to suppress again. When we suppress we are stopping the unconscious from becoming conscious.

Further, reacting to the sensation by suppressing is exhausting. Focusing our attention and energy on suppressing sensations means we don't have the mental space to focus elsewhere. It's like trying to hold a beachball under water. This means it takes longer to put together the presentation. When we do come to present, we are not able to enjoy the speaking opportunity. This is tiring and we go home exhausted and have no energy to spend quality time with our family.

Express

If it is not desirable to suppress sensations, perhaps you should express them? After all, we don't want to keep these sensations bottled up do we!

The ways we express the sensations in our body can range from our body language, to what we think, what we say and how we act. The purpose of expressing is to let out just enough of the undesirable sensation so we can then suppress what is left.

There are several problems with the strategy of expressing sensations. Perhaps you express to your boss that you don't want to do the presentation. The reasons you give only serve to reinforce to you your programming about presenting. If your boss hears you out and doesn't change their mind, you still have to revert to suppressing those sensations.

When we express, we often deliver it in the form of an attack. The energy with which we speak is undesirable and negative and our body language usually matches this. This is why we want to let it out. Unfortunately the person we are expressing our energy to will usually feel it as an attack – even if it is not. Have you ever had a partner come home and express how unfair a situation is at work? What did you feel about the energy?

Another way we express sensations is through worry. When we worry, we are trying to release the energetic sensations through a frame of catastrophising. We worry what could go wrong, what happens when it does and what the implications are. This leads people to experience the fallout from a bad presentation long before they stand to speak. As the 16th-century French philosopher Michel de Montaigne said, 'My life has been full of terrible misfortunes, most of which never happened.'

Expressing undesirable sensations is thought to be desirable because it feels very cathartic. We assume that it's good to do this. Freud is often cited as the one who gives us permission to express what we are feeling. While Freud was an early pioneer in the concept of catharsis, he stressed that it was important for the sensations to be 'talked out' with a trained professional as opposed to simply expressed into the void that is the world.

Possess

The strategies outlined above all relate to how we react to aversions. The way we react to cravings is a little more straightforward – we just want more of them. When we hold onto sensations they keep us locked in the past, or project us to an imaginary future. Some people do this with opportunities to present.

Perhaps you like speaking, and being front and centre gives you an adrenaline rush. For you, speaking to the senior leadership team is a marketing opportunity for your next promotion. For this reason we often like to hold onto the sensation we get when we think about presenting. We trigger these sensations by remembering how well we have presented in the past, the success we had and how that is all ahead of us again. After all, it feels good, and pop psychology says we should always think positive thoughts, right!

While this sounds reasonable, there are a few pitfalls to this strategy. First, if you crave a sensation too much you will develop an addiction to it. This is demonstrated in the second pitfall.

If you are thinking about the last time you presented and how well you went, you're not paying attention to your current situation. Being stuck in the past will not help you in the now. When you think of how good you were in the past, you may not see how things have changed and how your game has slipped. This can open you to not performing as well as you could.

* * *

When the sensory–body feedback loop gives our body a sensation to which we react with avoidance, suppression, expression or possession we are giving up control of our mindset. We become a slave to events that trigger the loop and those who know how to activate those sensations within us. This takes away our control of our life.

DO NOTHING IN ALL AREAS OF LIFE

The idea of not reacting to undesirable sensations makes sense. But what about desirable ones? What about the sensations we experience for those we love? Should we not react to those sensations too?

The answer to this is yes. If you've got teenagers, you'll know what I mean.

Remember when that teenager was a cute four year old? They came home from kindergarten one day and gave you a picture they had painted. The picture had you and them smiling next to the house, with a rainbow in the background. They gave it to you while explaining what they were thinking when they painted it. You then took the painting and stuck it to the wall where it stayed for years. It truly was a beautiful moment. You said you'd hold onto that love for the rest of your life. And you have.

Today, that four year old is a 15 year old. When they get home from school they walk through the door, grunt at you before drinking all the milk straight from the carton. They leave the fridge open as they head upstairs and spend the afternoon on social media with their friends.

You're flabbergasted. *What happened to that lovely four year old?* you wonder. *Where is the love and respect they once showed you? Why can't they be like they were?* You call them down and tell them that they should be more respectful, more engaging and more … like they were when they were four.

The reason they can't be that way is that four year old doesn't exist anymore, but you think they do. You're still holding on to the sensation that you had with them from 11 years ago. When they act the way they do today, it doesn't match what you remember happening. This produces a sensation you don't like and you react and become upset.

If, however, you had let go of the sensation from 11 years ago you would be able to see the uniquely beautiful experience that is a child as they metamorphise into an adult. It has its own beauty, but you'll miss it if you're looking for the four year old.

This holding on to past sensations happens in other relationships too. If we don't realise it and don't let that energy go we are headed for trouble. Just ask David.

What would happen if you let go of the love for your partner? If you love them, should you set them free? I think it is the only way.

If you remember back to David, after 23 years of being married to Caroline he was still holding onto the love they had over 20 years ago. But the love of the new relationship was long gone and only existed in his head. He was craving something that doesn't exist anymore. Because of this, he was missing the love that could be developed by two people committed to each other and their shared journey. This commitment creates a whole different type of love that has amazing beauty within it. But if you're holding onto a feeling from 20-plus years ago, you will see this current version of love as not as good as what you had back then.

The highest values of life are peace, joy and love. These sit behind everything in the universe. Every Teacher, Sage, Mystic, Avatar and Enlightened individual who has walked the earth has taught this. The Buddha said the only truth you can ever know is the truth as you experience it in your body. Christ said you shall know the truth and the truth shall set you free. Countless other enlightened people have said know thyself and the kingdom of heaven is within. Perhaps we should pay attention to what is going on in our body!

When we don't react to the energetic sensations we experience and let them deactivate themselves, we move towards peace, joy and love. We don't have to do anything to access this other than not react and observe the sensations that are being made conscious. If we hold on to the love of our partner from 20 years ago we are locking it in a place and time, stifling its ability to grow. However, when we deactivate it, over time it changes, grows and becomes the deepest version of itself. That is true deep love, something David was clearly missing out on.

But you can still enjoy life

Doing nothing does not mean not enjoying life's events. It means not reacting with cravings or aversions to them. When your child gives you a painting they created, be with them and listen to their story and enjoy their message. You can still put it on the wall and smile every time you see it. Experience the sensations it triggers in you without creating a story about those sensations. You avoid creating stories by applying the *Six Don'ts*.

HOW TO DO NOTHING

At its core, doing nothing is about experiencing a sensation as it rises and falls in your body. Be 100% present to it. Just observe the sensation and let yourself experience it. Do nothing about it.

When you observe it, notice what it does. Does it move up, down, left or right? Does it grow – if so, in what way? Does it want to sink into the depth of you, or to float up and away? Maybe it just sits there. Whatever it does, it does not mean anything. Just observe it.

This process is so simple that we make it hard. Every time I teach this in corporate courses people ask me, *how do I do nothing?* To be fair, it's a reasonable question. After all, they have spent their whole life not noticing the sensations in their body, and if they do, they have been encouraged to wrap a meaning around them. They were told to label them as though that would somehow help.

To assist with this doing nothing, I've developed the *Six Don'ts* to help you observe what is happening and let the energy move through your body. These have been designed to counter the well-intentioned bad advice we have all received from people who don't understand what causes sensations. These are the people who encourage us to hold onto feelings, label them to create a story, or simply ignore them if they are too hard to deal with.

> **Doing nothing is about experiencing a sensation as it rises and falls in your body.**

THE *SIX DON'TS*

Believe it or not, doing nothing can be pretty hard. We are so used to reacting and jumping to conclusions that we think it's a skill. It's not – it's simply a reaction based on cravings and aversions. Learning to not react is the skill. Below are the six most common sensations to *not* do so we don't get caught up in reactions that trigger the SBFL.

1. **Don't label.** Avoid labelling the sensation in any way. When we label a sensation with terms such as frustration, love, anger, excitement or anything else we are introducing a story. When we say, 'I am nervous about presenting,' we introduce a story based on a past experience that adds nothing of value to the current situation. It also brings in every other time we were nervous – including when we first learned to drive, asked out our high school sweetheart or lined up in the finals in our favourite sport. None of this is helpful at this time, and only serves to increase the noise in our head and the sensations in our body. This makes it harder to just observe.

2. **Don't own it.** We own a sensation when we say things like, 'This is just how I feel when I have to present.' This is playing victim to what we think has caused the sensation.

It disempowers us. It then draws us into the story of how this has happened in the past. When we are drawn into the past we are not observing.

3. **Don't judge it.** Don't make the sensation right or wrong. The classic example of this is, 'I should be more confident when I present.' When we assume we should feel different to the way we do it is just another thought the mind has generated in response to the body's aversion to the sensation. This in turn reactivates the SBFL and the process continues. The way we should feel is directed by the programming inside us, and that is what is happening. We don't know what programming is inside us so we can't say what way we should feel.

4. **Don't fight it.** When the sensation wants to come up, let it. Don't push it down. It may not be pleasant, but it is inside us. Until we let it come up and experience it, it will remain in us.

5. **Don't justify it.** When we justify our feeling of nervousness by saying, 'I should be nervous – this is a big presentation!' we are once again introducing a story. This enables the mind to go back to one of its many thought structures such as *life determines one's experiences* and whinge to the world. When we are caught in justifying we are caught in the thoughts around it and this does not allow us to experience the sensations.

6. **Don't explain it.** It's tempting to explain the way we feel with a story from the past: 'When I last presented to the SLT they tore me to shreds and that is why I feel this way.' Explaining allows us to be the victim and not have to take responsibility for how we are today. While we may have had a less than stellar experience last time, it serves no purpose now. It might remind us to prepare more thoroughly, but we can know we need to be well prepared without having to explain away the sensations we are experiencing.

As you're observing these sensations, know that nothing in the universe is permanent. Everything has a beginning, middle and end. This is true for the sensations in your body too. The sensations within you will rise and fall away. When you apply the *Six Don'ts* you are giving the sensations the best chance to be deactivated. This may take only 20 to 30 seconds, or as long as a few minutes, but it will follow that path and the trigger will be deactivated.

Applying the *Six Don'ts* is not about ignoring, avoiding or denying the sensations in any way. In fact it is the exact opposite. When you apply the *Six Don'ts* and just watch a sensation as it moves through your body you are giving 100% of your attention to it. This is what it wants.

When you pay attention to the energetic sensations in your body without reacting to them, you are making the unconscious conscious. You are getting to know the truth that is in your body, and when you know the truth, it shall set you free.

But how do I stop the thoughts?

Initially you won't be able to stop the thoughts triggered by the sensations from occurring. That will come with practice. The way you stop yourself becoming caught up in the thoughts is to simply focus on the sensations. You will still experience the thoughts in the background, but by focusing all your attention on the sensations you won't be drawn into them. When you do this, you are training your body to break out of the habit of reacting to the sensations with thoughts and the thoughts become less intrusive.

How do I know how well I am going?

There is quite a simple test to see how well you are going with not reacting. Take a moment to listen to the voice in your head. What is it talking about? If it is relatively quiet, or focusing on the tasks you have at hand, then you are well on the way to mastering you mindset. However, if it is still carrying on about something that happened earlier in the day, see if you can access the sensations the thoughts will be activating and experience them without becoming involved in the associated thoughts.

Rinse and repeat

When you experience a sensation, it's common for another one to take its place. It's like a game of whack-a-mole. This is not something going wrong. Rather it is just a deeper level of programming being activated in the recognising part of the sensory–body feedback loop and coming up to be made conscious. Once again, apply the *Six Don'ts* as you observe the sensations in your body.

HOLDING DOWN THE VOLCANO

When I first developed this exercise, I thought I'd try the technique out on a person with whom I had a particularly difficult relationship. Every time I spoke to them it ended in frustration and anger for both parties.

To practise not reacting to the sensations they triggered in me I sat at the kitchen table and thought of the person. As I did I could feel a sensation akin to a volcano erupting inside me. The sensation was white hot and wanted to explode into the sky. It was intense, and it was not very enjoyable. For a full five minutes I sat there experiencing the sensation and watching in my mind's eye what was happening. I simply watched it. I didn't label it or justify why I was feeling that way – and trust me, I had every reason to. I just watched and experienced it as it moved through my body.

After five minutes the lava explosion started to subside, and the sensation behind it receded. After another five minutes the sensation had dissipated.

After that 10-minute experience I thought of that person again. When I did, I didn't have any of the animosity towards them that I had just 11 minutes earlier. It wasn't a case of suddenly wanting to be their best friend – that was not the goal. I could think of them without reacting with an aversion and getting angry.

A week or so later I came across that person. To my pleasant surprise I didn't feel the tension and frustration that usually accompanied seeing them. I was able to be the better version of myself. I was able to deal with the business that needed to be attended to and move on.

In addition to that, I found they were more pleasant. It's not that what I did for me affected them – they were still acting the same way, but I wasn't being triggered by them. As a result we were both able to interact in a civilised manner and go our own way. To me that was a massive win.

When I reflected on how the changes had come about, it made sense. If every time I thought of that person I had to hold down a volcano within me, I'd have very little energy or attention to give to them. I would have projected out my white-hot anger and they would have reacted to it. There would have been no way we could have worked together. The added bonus of this is that when they projected their white-hot anger to me, I wasn't triggered by it. This meant a better and easier interaction for everyone involved.

WHAT IF YOU DON'T DO NOTHING?

Life continues as it has been and you become more of who you are.

When we react to sensations with either cravings or aversions, over time it changes our personality. The changes are small, but compound over time. If we keep reacting in the same way to the sensations, our reactions become habitual which in turn creates our personality. When we stop reacting our personality can change too. This changes how we perceive the world, and how people perceive us.

If we react to the sensations in any way we extend the refractory period. Instead of lasting only a few minutes, it could be extended up to a few hours or days. Have you ever come across a person who was in a bad mood all day – or all week – because something upset them on the way to work on Monday morning? That's a long refractory period!

If we keep reacting in the same way to the sensations, our reactions become habitual which in turn creates our personality.

In his book *Breaking the Habit of Being Yourself*, Dr Joe Dispenza explains how this compounds. When someone reacts with a craving or aversion they hold onto the sensation and create thoughts that create more of the same sensations. If they experience the sensation for long enough they develop a 'mood that they are in'. If they keep running the triggers and react to the sensations in the same way for long enough the mood turns to a temperament. *You've got to watch Jenny – she's always stressed at the end of the quarter!*

If we hold onto a temperament for long enough it becomes our familiar way of operating. We get to know how we will experience the sensations triggered by the environment and we can predict what we will experience during the day. There is comfort in the familiar, even if we don't outwardly like the feeling. When we act in accordance with our temperament for extended periods it becomes our personality. *Just stay away from Jenny – she's a grump.*

This is how people develop angry, fearful, sad, happy, excited or any other sort of personality. They are reacting to the sensations they experience as environmental triggers or memories of them and are 'stuck' reacting to them by not simply experiencing the sensations. We are usually not aware that this is what we are doing,

If you wish to change your personality, simply pay close attention to the sensations you experience in your body. When you do this you will change the way you react and this will change who you are.

CHAPTER 6
PUTTING MINDSET MASTERY TO WORK

In this book there is only one technique taught: don't react to the energetic sensations experienced in your body. This will help you make the unconscious conscious. This enables you to master your mindset and hold onto your mental peace and equanimity. It is a simple technique that can be used anywhere at any time while you are experiencing life. If you forget to implement it in real time, applying the technique after the event will still have fantastic results.

But being simple can often be a downfall of success. We tend to overlook the simple things, believing if it is simple it can't work. This chapter will show you how you can implement the technique in different situations so you can master your mindset.

THE $25,000 MIND TECHNIQUE

If you have just picked up this book and flipped straight to this page, welcome. Make sure you go back and read the pages leading to here. Knowing the why and how of the technique is just as important as doing it.

In 2011 I'd been working for the Australian Bureau of Statistics for five years. It was my job to count the number of people going to libraries, art galleries and museums. It wasn't as exciting as it sounds.

I'd been in the role for a number of years and had been overlooked for promotion many times. I'd looked at the people being promoted past me and wondered why they got promoted and I didn't.

During this time I'd also been developing my speaking and training practice as a side hustle. It had reached the point where I needed to make a decision about moving into it full time or to let it go and commit to counting library visitors for the rest of my career. With very little savings behind me and a regular paycheque coming from the ABS, leaving was proving harder than I wanted it to be.

Then one day I made the decision to leave and applied this mind technique below to make it happen. This technique works by severing the energetic connection you have with the person or entity you are trying to remove from your life. This technique may demonstrate to you how strong that connection is and why it has been difficult to sever it in the past. As this comes up, simply repeat the process until the real-world connection is broken.

1. Think of a person or thing that you'd like removed from your life. This is someone or something you don't want to have anything to do with again. For me, this was the ABS. For you it could be a person or substance (alcohol, nicotine, a property or car you want to sell – anything).

2. Sit in a chair, with your back straight, eyes closed. Take a few breaths through your nose and feel the air pass over the skin.

3. In your mind's eye, picture that person or thing in front of you. For me, I represented the ABS by picturing the building I went to work in each day.

4. In your mind's eye, see a connection from your naval to the person or object you are trying to leave. This connection will be made of whatever it is made of. It could be rope, chain, cable, dental floss or anything else. When I did this with the ABS, I pictured a rope coming from my naval and going around the 20-storey building.

5. In your mind's eye, picture the connection being cut. This may be harder than it sounds. It might take some determined effort. You might also find that you have a butter knife trying to cut a thick rope. Whatever it is, keep cutting. If needed, see if you can change what you are using to something

sharper. You may not be able to. You may also find that when you cut the connection it instantly reconnects. If it does, just keep cutting it.

6. Observe any sensations that arise when you're trying to sever the connection.

7. Apply the *Six Don'ts* to them. Don't label them, don't own them, don't judge them, don't fight them, don't justify them, and don't explain the sensations. Just watch the energetic sensations in your body.

8. When you have cut the connection, watch the person or thing float off into the distance until it disappears.

9. As it floats away, repeat silently to yourself, 'I release you in perfect and profitable ways,' or, 'I release you in perfect and loving ways.' Or some variation of this. You want to send the message that you are releasing them, and you may as well be loving and profitable or perfect in it.

10. As it disappears, observe the sensations that come up in your body.

11. Apply the *Six Don'ts* to them.

12. Repeat the above steps three times per sitting.

13. Watch to see what turns up in your world. The world will send you signals for you to follow. These signals could be anything, and are usually completely out of the blue, but so accurate for what you need to know or do. It's your job to pay attention to them and act accordingly. You'll know what they are when they show up. As these signals are presented to you, it will activate sensations within your body. Don't react to them – just watch them as they exist in your body and take the action you deem appropriate.

14. Repeat the whole process as often as you can – potentially several times a day – until the person or thing is removed from your life.

It is important to keep your outer world actions congruent with your inner world intentions. If you are wanting to remove a person from your life, don't do the technique and then pick up the phone and call them. If you're trying to leave an organisation, don't apply for a promotion or transfer within it. If you do this, you are sending a mixed signal to the universe.

Over the Easter weekend of 2011 I repeated this technique four times a day, to help me leave the ABS. When I returned to the office after Easter, a strange thing happened. Somehow I managed to get into an intense conversation with my Director. Somehow we managed to start discussing why I had not been promoted. He suggested I had not shown enough ability to analyse data. When I pointed to a recently published article, he came up with another excuse. When I countered that with evidence to the contrary, he came up with another reason.

After a few reasons I said to him that he was deliberately holding me back. At this point he said that yes he was. He and the leadership team had made a decision that I was never to be promoted, and that I had only three options. I could stay where I was, I could leave, or I could wait until there was a change in the leadership team and see if the new person viewed me differently.

I suggested there was a fourth option – they could retrench me! I had never thought of this option until this moment.

He admitted that he had not thought of this option either as there was a public service wide ban on redundancies, but he said he would look into it.

Over the weeks as we negotiated the settlement, I remember feeling the sense of frustration and unfairness of the situation, but also the excitement of what was happening. I was finally leaving a place that I knew was against me and was about to jump full time into my dream career. As I felt these sensations I just observed them as they moved through my body. This was particularly hard in some situations, but by paying attention to what was happening I was able to remain centred in my body and not react to what I was experiencing.

A few weeks later the paperwork was signed and I received $25,000 to leave. I then jumped full time into my practice and haven't looked back.

A QUICK CALIBRATION

I'm now going to step you through a series of different situations for which you can use the Mindset Mastery technique to achieve outcomes you are after. But first, it's a good idea to gain an understanding of how strong the sensations are within you in relation to these situations with a quick calibration. For each technique below, it's a good idea to take a calibration both before and after to determine the strength of the sensation. Doing this is relatively simple and only takes a few moments. Taking a calibration also makes it easier to detect and not react to the sensations.

Back in chapter 2 under the heading of *How to observe sensations*, we looked at a simple body scan you can perform. This gave you a path to examine the energetic sensations we all experience in our body. Performing a calibration is just a matter of tapping into those sensations and determining how strong they are. Follow these steps to perform a calibration:

1. Think of the situation that causes an undesirable energetic sensation in you.
2. Identify any physical sensations you experience. Don't label them. Use physical descriptions such as shaking, heavy, tight,

weight on shoulders, sinking in stomach – as opposed to fear, apprehension, and so on.

3. Rate the intensity of these sensations out of 10, with 10 being the highest. Do not use the value seven. Seven is a cop out where we can be not committed either way. If you want to rate a sensation as a seven, decide if it is either a six or eight.

OVERCOMING IMPOSTER SYNDROME

Imposter syndrome is one of the most common ailments my clients speak about. Many very senior leaders, experts and accomplished professionals doubt their ability and worth to do what they are often highly paid to do.

And it's not just business people who report this. Successful sports stars, actors, entrepreneurs, artists, musicians, parents and even authors report feeling as though they are a fraud and that someone else would be better doing what they do. If you read almost any biography of someone who has been successful you will see a story of someone overcoming imposter syndrome. The fact that you are feeling it means you're just like the rest of us.

But knowing you're just like the rest of us doesn't always make the feeling any easier to deal with, or make it go away. Imposter syndrome arises when you are at the edge of your comfort zone. This is a good thing as it means you are growing. The way that most people are encouraged to overcome this feeling is to feel the fear and do it anyway. Or to just trust yourself. Or harden up. Or just ignore the feelings. But this doesn't work. If it did, we'd have moved on from it years ago.

Here is the Mindset Mastery way to overcome imposter syndrome:

1. Identify a situation where you feel the sense of being an imposter come on. This could be speaking up in a meeting,

picking up the phone to make a sales call or applying for a promotion.

2. Access the sensations in your body that you experience in this situation. Be fully present to the energetic sensations that arise when the trigger is encountered.
3. Calibrate the intensity of the sensations you feel.
4. Apply the *Six Don'ts* to them. Don't label them, don't own them, don't judge them, don't fight them, don't justify them, and don't explain the sensations. Just watch the energetic sensation in your body.
5. Repeat until the sensation has been deactivated.

You can use this technique in real time during a meeting if you remember, or at a later date. Either way is fine.

MAKING SALES CALLS

There is something about cold calls that sends most salespeople into hiding. Countless books have been written on the art of these calls and how to make them enjoyable. Authors suggest scripts to get past gatekeepers, offer advice on developing the ideal elevator pitch and provide expert advice on dealing with the fear of rejection. If the usual strategies don't work, we are encouraged to just 'smile and dial' as we push through the pain.

But we've all been called by someone either just going through the motions or forcing themselves to make the call. We pick up on their energy and the call doesn't last long. It's a waste of everyone's time

In a poll I ran on LinkedIn surveying over 100 salespeople, 43.5% of respondents said that making cold calls was the hardest part of their role. A further 17.4% said that asking for the order was. This means that 61% of salespeople find doing the most basic parts of their role stressful.

However, if you know your script and the value you offer to the prospect and you're calling targeted prospects who need what you have, nothing should be stressful.

But like all things in life, whether we like it or not depends purely on the story we tell ourselves. These stories are based on the energetic sensations we experience when we think of the task. If when we think of cold calling or asking for the order we get a sensation that we find undesirable, we won't make the calls.

So to be more accurate, it is not the cold calls that people don't like. Rather, it's the sensation in their body that they experience when they have to make them that they don't like. No amount of scripting, smiling and dialling or just forcing our way through will overcome the sensation. If salespeople want to stop cold calling being something they find stressful they have to deactivate the sensations they experience when they make the calls. Here are the steps on how to do this:

1. Prepare a list of prospects.
2. Look at the list and pay attention to the sensation as it arises within you.
3. Calibrate the intensity of the sensations you feel.
4. Observe the sensations and what they do. Apply the *Six Don'ts*.
5. Identify a prospect to call. Imagine making the call and what you will say. Observe any sensations that arise in your body.
6. Apply the *Six Don'ts* to them. Don't label them, don't own them, don't judge them, don't fight them, don't justify them, and don't explain the sensations. Just watch the sensations in your body.

7. Make the call. While on the phone, pay attention to any energetic sensations you experience in your body. Apply the *Six Don'ts* to them.
8. After the call, reflect on the call and how it went. Apply the *Six Don'ts* to any energetic sensation that arises.
9. Perform another calibration of the sensations you experience and determine their value. You should have noticed a reduction in the severity. Be aware that you may now experience a new or different sensation in its place. If you do, repeat the process.

With this technique it is important to note that you are not looking for an energetic sensation you would rate as desirable. You are not looking to make cold calling fun. This would just be a craving that needs to be deactivated. All you are looking to do is observe any sensations that arise so you can experience them without reacting.

THAT PERSON WHO PISSES YOU OFF

We all have them. They might be colleagues, your boss or a client you have to deal with. It could be a sibling or in-law – hopefully you're not married to them! It could be someone on the school committee, at your sporting club or your partner's best friend.

Whoever it is, you know who I mean. They are people who don't have to do anything and yet they annoy you. It could be something as superficial as how they carry themselves with an air of arrogance, neediness or excessive fake sincerity. Whoever they are, they have a message for you.

When someone annoys you it is simply a program being activated within you. That program represents a part of you that you have not fully integrated. It was Carl Jung who said that if we want to be fully whole individuals we need to integrate these repressed parts. He called them the Shadow. When someone annoys you, they are simply activating a Shadow element of your personality. They are showing you exactly where you need to work so you can make the unconscious conscious. This is how you do it:

1. When you encounter that annoying person, pay attention to the energetic sensations that arise in your body.
2. Apply the *Six Don'ts* to them. Don't label them, don't own them, don't judge them, don't fight them, don't justify them, and don't explain the sensations. Just watch the sensations in your body.
3. Repeat this process as often as you need to when you are around this person.

If you are unable to deactivate in their presence – or you forget – that's not a problem. Simply sit down, close your eyes and think of them. As the memory of them activates sensations within you, simply apply the *Six Don'ts* and watch as the sensation dissipates. This will work just as well as doing it in real time.

You can also apply this technique before going to see someone you know will trigger you, such as the dentist or the in-law you don't get along with.

THAT DRINK WHEN I GET HOME

'It's just one drink, and I only have it to unwind and let go of the stress of the day. How bad can it be?'

It's a common refrain of workers right across Australia. While the Australian Institute of Health and Welfare report that the overall consumption of alcohol is falling, it is still the most detected drug in wastewater. It's not my place to debate how bad a single drink is, but health professionals who know a lot about this tell me that there are lots of people who want to kick the habit.

A faux relaxant

Alcohol is often consumed under the guise of helping us relax. On the surface it seems to do that. When we've had a glass or two we no longer feel the stresses of the day and we think we are relaxed. However, this is not the case.

Alcohol is a numbing agent. It interferes with our ability to feel our body and detect and process the signals from it. If you've ever woken up injured after a big night out and you don't remember how it happened, you'll know what I mean. Even a small amount of alcohol numbs us to our mind–body instrument. This means you feel less. You then interpret this as being relaxed. But you're not.

The problem of using alcohol to 'relax' is the programming that causes us to assess something as stressful is not deactivated. This means that while we might feel better for a short period and we interpret this as relaxing, all we are doing is masking what is going on. We will still have the stress the following day, except it will be slightly worse as the body is now processing alcohol.

Deactivating the drive for that one glass follows the same process as all other deactivations. However, it should be conducted before any alcohol is consumed:

1. The desire for a drink is usually triggered by a specific event. It could be leaving the office, walking through the front door, seeing the clock turn over to 5 pm, starting the preparation for dinner or putting the kids to bed. Whatever it is, identify the context that triggers the desire for a drink in you.
2. In your mind's eye, imagine yourself encountering the event that causes the trigger.

3. Be fully present to the energetic sensations that arise when the trigger is encountered.
4. Calibrate the strength of the sensations.
5. Apply the *Six Don'ts* to them. Don't label them, don't own them, don't judge them, don't fight them, don't justify them, and don't explain the sensations. Just watch the sensations in your body.
6. Repeat three times.
7. Recalibrate the sensations to determine any reduction in intensity. You should have noticed a reduction in the severity. Be aware that you may now experience a new or different sensation in its place. If you do, repeat the process.

In addition to the above deactivation you may find it useful to have another drink available such as soda water or water. This will help take care of the physical thirst you may be feeling.

MAKING MONEY WORK

When I was a kid I grew up in a house with no money. Mum and Dad had set up an airline in Wangaratta in country Victoria that didn't go well. Their plan was to ferry passengers down to Melbourne and across the state and they believed they could make some good money out of it. While on paper the business idea made a lot of sense, unfortunately planes don't fly on paper. After some initial success, debts mounted up and Mum and Dad were declared bankrupt. I was six at the time.

Part of the process of bankruptcy was they lost everything, including the house. As they both worked in the business, neither of them had a job or savings to fall back on. I got to see this close up. I remember coming home from school on two occasions to find the man from St Vincent de Paul at the kitchen table taking a shopping order so we could eat that week. My older brother had a paper run. There were times when my parents borrowed money from him so we could eat. Things were pretty dire. Dad moved to Sydney to find work while Mum and I and my three siblings stayed behind, living off handouts.

After we all moved to Sydney, it took three years for the bankruptcy to be discharged, a further four for their names to be cleared so they could then borrow money to buy a house again, and a total of 10-plus years to get back to square one.

With this type of programming in childhood, it was no wonder that when I went out into the world I didn't have any idea how to attract enough money to get ahead in life. I knew how to budget what little I had (Mum drilled that into us), but as far as getting enough to get by on, I had no idea.

Through my strong budgeting I was very good at saving, but something very frustrating would happen. If I managed to save a few hundred dollars, I'd be hit with a bill that just happened to match what was in the bank. I remember at one stage I had saved just over $500 and I was pretty happy with myself. I was planning a holiday with my girlfriend. But the day after I got to that figure I received three bills and a speeding fine that came to just shy of $500.

This happened continually for close to 20 years. It did not matter where I lived, what sort of job I had or what my relationship status was. Month after month I was always short of cash. As the late Jim Rohn would say, there is always too much month at the end of the money.

It wasn't that I didn't know how to manage money, it was that I wasn't taking the opportunity to release the programming I had around it when it turned up. Every time I received a bill (or fine) and I felt the sensation from it, I reacted by suppressing it so I didn't have to deal with it. I now know that all I was doing was stopping the unconscious becoming conscious. This meant I would be driven to make decisions that meant I would create a situation where the sensation could come up again. It was a life pattern I was trapped in. It took me more than 20 years to learn this lesson. If you can relate to this example, try the following technique and save yourself a bunch of time and stress:

1. Identify an aspect of your finances that triggers you. It might be your bank account, your credit card statement, a personal loan, your mortgage or calls from debt collectors.
2. As you think of this trigger, watch the energetic sensations within your body.
3. Calibrate those sensations.
4. Apply the *Six Don'ts* to them. Don't label them, don't own them, don't judge them, don't fight them, don't justify them, and don't explain the sensations. Just watch the sensations in your body.
5. Repeat the process as often as required for the trigger.
6. Recalibrate the sensations to determine any reduction in intensity. You should have noticed a reduction in the severity. Be aware that you may now experience a new or different sensation in its place. If you do, repeat the process.
7. Systematically work through other areas of money and finance and experience any energetic sensations associated with them. The more areas you deactivate the more programming you will release.

It doesn't get you out of consequences

Deactivating the energetic sensations around money won't help you avoid the consequences of past decisions. What is done is done and we must all bear the consequences of our decisions. What it will give you is the ability to make different choices in the future. This will enable you to create different outcomes that you will find more favourable.

Remember, all of life is impermanent. At some time in the future your financial position will be different.

DROP 20 KILOS

When I started working with Jason he was in a bad shape. In his early 50s, he'd found that his blood glucose was constantly over 12, his diabetes was out of control and he was carrying an extra 40 kilos spread evenly around his waist, neck and backside. Working at a very senior level in one of Australia's largest companies, he just thought that this was the price of success. But Jason knew if he kept up this lifestyle he was headed for an early grave.

The real problem for Jason was that he knew what he had to do to correct the situation, but he wasn't doing it. He just needed to visit the doctor, take advice on adjusting his lifestyle and follow it. He knew this, but didn't do it.

Jason was like a lot of males of his vintage – not accustomed to visiting the doctor. When he thought of going, he had an undesirable energetic sensation that he wanted to avoid, so he did.

To enable him to improve his health, we deactivated the energetic sensations he experienced when he thought of visiting the doctor. After the deactivation, Jason was able to visit the doctor without the usual aversions. When he was there he was able to share more honestly and fully what she needed to know. The doctor gave him a list of things to start and stop doing. He started visiting a psychologist to give insights to manage relationships, a nurse to manage his diabetes and he even got a personal trainer to help him exercise.

After six months his blood pressure was down to almost normal levels, he'd dropped 20 kilos and his blood glucose levels were starting to come under control. Jason knows he still has a way to go, but he can now do it as he is not fighting against himself when he thinks about the doctor.

Deactivating the energetic sensations associated with the doctor follows the same process as any other deactivation:

1. Think of visiting the doctor.
2. Observe any energetic sensations that arise in your body.
3. Calibrate the strength of the sensations.
4. Apply the *Six Don'ts* to them. Don't label them, don't own them, don't judge them, don't fight them, don't justify them, and don't explain the sensations. Just watch the sensations in your body.
5. Recalibrate the strength of the sensations to determine any reduction in intensity. You should have noticed a reduction in the severity. Be aware that you may now experience a new or different sensation in its place. If you do, repeat the process.
6. Repeat as necessary.

BACK TO SLEEP AT 3 AM

Constantly waking up at 3 am and ruminating on some trivial aspect of the last 24 hours is no fun. It can be particularly stressful when it's ruminating on something serious that needs to be addressed. But to be able to address it properly the following day, you need a good night's sleep – something that can be elusive.

When we have too many nights of waking up at 3 am and not being able to get back to sleep, going to bed becomes stressful. Instead of being able to unwind and relax at bedtime, we can feel tension rise and fear of another night awake mounts. This makes going to sleep even harder. You can lessen the impact of this by not reacting to the sensation of waking at 3 am:

1. When you wake in the middle of the night, pay attention to the sensations in and on your body. The sensations in your body are a result of the SBFL. The sensations on your body will include your body lying on the bed, your head on the pillow and the blankets on your body. Also pay attention to any sensations you experience when you think the thoughts that are keeping you awake. Focus on the sensations, not the thoughts.

2. Pay close attention to these sensations.

3. Apply the *Six Don'ts* to them. Don't label them, don't own them, don't judge them, don't fight them, don't justify them, and don't explain the sensations. Just watch the sensations in your body.

My experience with this technique is that it usually takes less than a minute to go back to sleep.

CHOCOLATE BE GONE

This technique will work for any vice you feel drawn to. It could be lollies, alcohol, cake, TV watching or any other guilty pleasure you enjoy. In this example we will use chocolate.

Use this technique when you know you will have to be around a trigger but don't want to be triggered by it. Chocolate is common in society for social gatherings, morning teas and in the supermarket. No matter how hard you try to avoid it, it will pop up somewhere in your week. This technique will deactivate the sensations within you that draw you to it:

1. Decide you want to be rid of the attraction to chocolate.

2. Sit comfortably with your back straight and eyes closed. Focus on the air coming in and out of your nose for a few breaths.
3. Picture in your mind's eye the chocolate you want to break your attraction to. It might be a specific type of chocolate bar, a certain block of chocolate or a box containing an assortment of chocolate bars. For me it was honeycomb.
4. Calibrate the strength of the sensations.
5. While thinking about the chocolate, pay attention to any sensations that arise in your body. Watch them.
6. Apply the *Six Don'ts* to them. Don't label them, don't own them, don't judge them, don't fight them, don't justify them, and don't explain the sensations. Just watch the sensations in your body.
7. When the sensations have subsided, think of another version of chocolate and repeat the process. This is usually enough to break the temptation.
8. Recalibrate the sensations to determine any reduction in intensity. You should have noticed a reduction in the severity. Be aware that you may now experience a new or different sensation in its place. If you do, repeat the process.

Testing your success

The steps above are usually enough to deactivate the desire for chocolate, but it's good to test this out. The steps below are how you can test yourself to know how well the deactivation worked.

1. Visit the shop and buy your favourite chocolate.
2. With the packet still closed, look at the chocolate, feel it, and see if you can smell the chocolate through the wrapping.
3. Observe any sensations that arise in your body.

4. Apply the *Six Don'ts* to them. Don't label them, don't own them, don't judge them, don't fight them, don't justify them, and don't explain the sensations. Just watch the sensations in your body.
5. Over the next few days, leave the chocolate in its wrapper in a place where you will regularly see it. Observe any sensations that arise in your body as you see it. Apply the *Six Don'ts*.
6. After a week, open the packet and smell the chocolate. Again, release any sensations that arise in your body.
7. Leave the chocolate open on a plate in a place where you will regularly see it. Observe any sensations that arise in your body as you see and smell it over the days it is open.
8. After a week, take a bite of the chocolate. Enjoy the taste and sensations that arise in your body as you enjoy the flavour. Let the sensations go.

If you follow this process you will very quickly get to the point where you can have chocolate in your house and you are not immediately drawn to consume it. This process will work for any vice you are attracted to. If you wish to use this technique for alcohol, it is advisable to use this before you consume any. Alcohol is a numbing agent and you simply won't feel any sensations in your body.

MEN IN BLACK – MEMORY ERASING

In the 1997 movie *Men in Black* aliens had started populating Earth. It was the job of the Men in Black to keep this a secret from the humans so no one was scared. If a human saw an alien the Men in Black would be deployed to take care of the situation. They gathered those who had seen the alien and ask them to look at a 'neuraliser'. A bright light would flash and this would isolate the electrical impulses in the brain and delete any memory of the aliens. I always thought that it would be cool to have one of them. I'd then be able to erase a heap of memories of the dumb things I'd done.

Turns out, I didn't need the expensive (and non-existent) toy as I had an inbuilt neuraliser in my body! This is how you use it:

1. Think of a memory that you'd like to erase.
2. Calibrate the strength of the sensations associated with it.
3. Sit in a chair with your back straight. Close your eyes and take a few breaths through your nose.
4. Replay the memory that you'd like to erase.
5. As you are replaying the memory, pay attention to any sensations in your body. Just watch them.
6. Apply the *Six Don'ts* to them. Don't label them, don't own them, don't judge them, don't fight them, don't justify them, and don't explain the sensations. Just watch the sensations in your body.
7. Repeat the process three times.
8. Move on and do something else.
9. Avoid reprogramming. If you sit and try to remember the memory you've just tried to erase, it will be reprogrammed into you. Get up and move away so you are distracted from that memory. You will find that within a few minutes you will have forgotten the memory.
10. Several hours after this, see if you can access the memory. Calibrate any sensations experienced in relation to them. You should have noticed a reduction in the severity. Be aware that you may now experience a new or different sensation in its place. If you do, repeat the process.

This technique has been useful for me in a few situations. When my youngest daughter was six we went to the shops. She was riding her scooter and I was walking alongside her. As she was racing along in full control she hit a small rock with her front wheel. At that moment the scooter stopped dead in its tracks and she was launched over the handle bars, landing head first onto the pavement. As she was wearing a helmet and not crying, I encouraged her to get up. She got up and screamed, 'My teeth!'

As I looked at her angelic face I saw her two front teeth smashed in half. As I registered this I felt a huge sensation rush through my body. It was like I was being electrocuted. I sprang into action. I called my dentist at the shops we were headed to. Dr Trilock stayed open to perform his magic. Within 45 minutes of the accident he had repaired her teeth. Looking at Addie's teeth today, you wouldn't know that they were half fake.

But my recovery from this took a lot longer. More than 10 years after the event, if I recalled the accident I would still experience the energetic sensation I felt on the day. Seeing my beautiful daughter with her teeth smashed in was something I thought I would never forget. That was until I deactivated the memory.

Now when I think of the event I only have a minor reaction to it. If I wanted to, I could deactivate this further. The reason I don't is I need to remember it to speak about it!

I have also used this technique to erase other traumatic memories. I was once told of the tragic workplace death of someone who was once very dear to me. When I received the call, I had the typical severe reaction – the energetic sensation equivalent of being hit with a cricket bat. As I replayed that call over the afternoon, I continued to experience the same sensation.

A few hours after the phone call I decided to deactivate the sensation. I sat with the sensation and watched as it moved through my body. This took a few minutes, but it eventually subsided. I could then think of the call without the same energetic reaction.

It's important to know that this erasing of the reaction to the memory didn't downplay or nullify any of the grief I felt about the death. What it enabled me to do was to be more fully present to the grief I was feeling and process it without reliving the sensation shock of the phone call.

YOU 2.0

If you've ever had a goal of developing a certain quality, this technique is for you.

Perhaps the goal is to be more generous. Or maybe more relaxed, or more loving with your partner, or more present when playing with your children. Whatever it is, this will help:

1. Identify a characteristic you'd like to develop.
2. Identify what a person with that characteristic would do. If it is being more generous, it might be giving a few dollars to a homeless person on the way to work. If it is being more loving to your partner, it might be giving them a bunch of flowers.
3. Sit in a chair with your back straight. Close your eyes and take a few breaths through your nose.
4. In your mind's eye, picture yourself doing an activity that someone with the characteristic you want would do. In the example of being more generous, it might be giving $5 to someone on the street asking for it.
5. Calibrate any sensations you experience in your body.
6. Apply the *Six Don'ts* to them. Don't label them, don't own them, don't judge them, don't fight them, don't justify them,

and don't explain the sensations. Just watch the sensations in your body.

7. Repeat the process three times.

Now 10× it

This part of the technique will boost the effectiveness of the above:

1. While sitting in the chair, picture yourself increasing the characteristic by a factor of 10.
2. Picture yourself giving $50 to someone on the street asking for it.
3. Observe and calibrate any sensations in your body.
4. Apply the *Six Don'ts* to the sensations.
5. Repeat the process three times.
6. Recalibrate any sensations you experience in your body around this characteristic you wish to develop. You should notice a reduction in the severity. Be aware that you may now experience a new or different sensation in its place. If you do, repeat the process.
7. Go out into the world and act in a generous way.
8. Observe any sensations in your body. Apply the *Six Don'ts* to the sensations.

Does this mean that you have to give $5 to every person who asks for it? No, but you can if you want. This is about acting from a position of choice.

Prior to this technique you would not have given $5 because of the programming inside you. The energetic sensation you experience would have told you to not do it. Now you can make a decision to give to the person or not from a position of choice. This could include simply not wanting to, needing the money for a coffee or something else.

DEEP CONCENTRATION

We all have times when we need to have deep concentration to do the deep work required of our role. If we can't get into the right mindset to concentrate, any task will take more of our time, attention and energy than it should. If you need to develop deep concentration, this technique is for you:

1. Identify the activity that requires your deep attention.
2. Sit in a chair with your back straight. Close your eyes and take a few breaths through your nose.
3. In your mind's eye, picture yourself working on that task. You can picture it from your point of view, or as though you are watching yourself do it. Either is fine.
4. Observe any sensations that arise in your body.
5. Calibrate the sensations.
6. Apply the *Six Don'ts* to them. Don't label them, don't own them, don't judge them, don't fight them, don't justify them, and don't explain the sensations. Just watch the sensations in your body.
7. Continue to watch the scene for a few minutes, constantly observing the sensations in your body.
8. Recalibrate any sensations you experience in your body around this characteristic you wish to develop. You should notice a reduction in the severity. Be aware that you may now experience a new or different sensation in its place. If you do, repeat the process.

9. Go off and work on the task. You should find fewer distractions and a greater ability to focus on achieving your goals.

I used this exercise every morning while writing this book. I was able to get four to five hours of solid concentration each day from this one technique.

DECISION MAKING

Often we need to make a decision between two equally valid options. Even after going through all your decision-making frameworks and processes you may find that there still isn't much between the two options.

What should you do?

The usual process is to weigh up what will be the best way to proceed. However, as we have seen earlier in the book, when we weigh up options it is just the one voice talking to itself. The voice is not impartial or independent. What the Voice is measuring against is not always the decisions and their outcomes.

What the Voice is weighing up is how it will feel inside if either option is selected. It is testing its programming on how it will feel when it encounters each situation. It will then select the option that will give it the more desirable sensation. This will not always give you the best outcome for the situation.

There is a better way:

1. Sit in a chair with your back straight. Close your eyes and take a few breaths through the nose. Pay attention to the air passing over the skin and as it moves in and out of your nostrils.
2. Hold in your mind option 1. As you do, pay attention to the sensations that arise in your body.

3. Apply the *Six Don'ts* to them. Don't label them, don't own them, don't judge them, don't fight them, don't justify them, and don't explain the sensations. Just watch the sensations in your body.
4. When the sensations have subsided, repeat the process with the second option.
5. Repeat the process three times and the solution should become clear.
6. If at the end of this process you are still not clear on the best decision to make, repeat the process again, but hold each option in your mind for longer and longer periods of time.
7. If after repeating the process a number of times you are still unable to see the obvious choice, perhaps there is another option that needs to be investigated. Repeat the above process, this time holding in your mind that you have chosen neither option 1 nor 2. Let go of any sensations that arise from this.

CONCLUSION

LIVING 100% IN CHOICE

NOW WHAT?

Mindset Mastery can be a great intellectual exercise that is fun to play with. But unless you put it into action, you won't have gained much. So go take action. Take action that will move you towards the goals you are after. When you feel sensations in your body, don't react to them – just observe them without creating any cravings or aversions about them.

As you are taking action, pay attention to what shows up in your world. It could be things that help or hinder and what you want to achieve. Whatever it is, observe what happens as the world around you triggers the sensation within you, and don't react. Take action if appropriate, but don't react. Watch that energy as it moves through your body and apply the *Six Don'ts* to it.

When we approach any situation without any preconceived stories about what we should expect, we can see what is truly there. This will trigger ever deeper programming in us and experience the sensations without reaction so we can deactivate them. Not only is that the path to being able to concentrate and be more productive at work, it is also the path to spiritual enlightenment.

WHAT ABOUT DAVID?

If there is a downside to Mindset Mastery it is that you are now living in 100% choice for your life. You can't blame anyone for anything. Ever. You are responsible for all of your thoughts, decisions and actions. You can't blame an affair on the feeling you had and how it just 'felt right'. This is just programming inside you about a craving you have.

When I showed an early copy of this manuscript to a friend, he challenged me about David having his affair with Nicole. He asked, 'If David had used this technique, can you be 100% certain he would have avoided the affair?'

The answer to that has to be *no*. We always have free choice. We can choose to do what we want to do, or we can choose to not do it.

What Mindset Mastery would have given him is a clearer insight into what he could or should do next. Perhaps his marriage to Caroline was not what he was after and Nicole was. Perhaps he really loved Caroline to a deep level but had been holding onto a 20-year-old story and he needed to meet Nicole to realise this.

But if David was using the Mindset Mastery technique he would have been acting free from any story he had made up. He would have been able to understand that the sensations in his body didn't mean he *had* to have an affair. Rather he would have known that the sensations were just the result of programming being activated inside him. He could have watched and enjoyed the sensation in his body without acting on it and gone home to Caroline. Or home with Nicole.

But he would have been acting from choice and known what he was doing. Or not doing.

When you think about it, it's pretty amazing that you can meet someone and they trigger amazing energies within you that make you feel such wonderful sensations such as joy, and love. But if you act on this when you don't really want to, that joy and love can easily turn into an expensive divorce – the exact opposite of what you were chasing.

When you use Mindset Mastery you act from a position of choice. You are not run by your subconscious programming. You are free to choose how you feel, how you act and what you do or don't do.

This means you can live a life free of habits, free of relying on discipline and free of needing something external to you to control what you do. You will be free of reactive behaviour and can avoid the mess that usually follows. In other words, you can do less and achieve more. That is what Mindset Mastery is about.

REFERENCES

Bond, N. & McConkey, K. *Psychological Science: An introduction*

Carnegie, D. *How to Win Friends and Influence People*

Clear, J. *Atomic Habits*

Coelho, P. *The Alchemist*

Cook, P. *New Rules of Management*

Duhigg, C. *The Power of Habits*

Eyal, N. *InDistractable*

Eysenck, M. *Principles of Cognitive Psychology*

Feist & Feist, *Theories of Personality, 5th edition*

Filo, R.V.T. 'Hermann Rorschach: From klecksography to psychiatry'

Fogg, B.J. *Tiny Habits*

Greene, R. *48 Laws of Power*

Greene, R. *The Art of Seduction*

Grey, W. & LaViolette, P. 'Feeling Codes and Organized Thinking'

Hart, W. *The Art of Living*

Hawkins, Dr. *Truth vs Falsehood: The art of spiritual discernment*

Hawkins, Dr. *Power vs Force: The hidden determinants of human behaviour*

Hawkins, Dr. *Letting Go*

Jeffers, S. *Feel the Fear and Do It Anyway*

Jung, C. *Archetypes and the Collective Unconscious*

Kahneman, D. *Thinking Fast and Slow*

Koga, F. & Kishimi, I. *The Courage to be Disliked*

Manson, M. *The Subtle Art of Not Giving a F*ck*

McRaven, W. *Make Your Bed*

Singer, M. *The Untethered Soul*

Vaden, R. *Take the Stairs*

van der Kolk, B. 'The Body Keeps the Score; Brain, mind and body in the healing of Trauma'

For more useful references and resources, go to
www.darrenfleming.com.au/mmresources

INDEX

$25,000 mind technique 80–83
10× it 102–103

A

acceptance 12
aches and pains 28
acting from choice 5
addiction 7, 67
affirmations 7
alcohol xiii, 64, 81, 89–91, 96, 98
anger 5, 12, 71, 74, 75, 88–89
apathy 11–12, 49
apps xi
atoms 18–19
aversions 5, 7, 9–12, 10, 14–15, 30, 63–66
avoiding xvi, 21, 25, 53, 63–64, 64, 73

B

being right 39–40
being wrong 39–40
blame 38, 51, 108
body language 65, 66
body scan 26–29, 84
Brown, Brené 23, 25, 64
Buddha 9–11, 69

C

calibration 84–85
change 10–11
chocolate 29, 96–98
choices xiv, 2–4, 94, 107–109
cognising 6
commitment 48–49
conflict xiii, 64
control 18–21
countering xv–xvi
cravings 5, 7, 9–12, 14–15, 29, 30, 35–36, 39, 66–67

D

David and Nicole 2–4, 14, 25, 69, 108–109

decision making 104–105
deep concentration 103–104
default mode network 34
deficit perspective xi
diet xiii–xvii, 35–36, 41, 96–97
different ways of thinking xi–xviii
digestive sensations 28
discipline xi–xviii, 109
  the problem with xii–xvi
Dispenza, Dr Joe 76
doing nothing 59–75
dreams xii
drugs 64, 89
due-date strategy 21–22

E

energetic sensations xv–xvi, 5, 7
  avoiding 5–15
  experiencing 5–15, 22–24, 26–30, 74
  focusing on 13
  labelling 12, 23–25, 71–72
  overriding xv–xvi
  purpose of xv–xvi
  reacting to xvi, 5–12, 68–70, 74
  stories and 50–54
  thoughts and 38–39
  ways of dealing with 21–30
energy 17–30
equanimity xvi–xvii, 4–5, 8–12, 14, 15, 49, 80
  killers of 4–5
evolution xv, 7
expressing 65–66
external stimuli xvi, 28
Eyal, Nir 64

F

fate xv
fear 23–24
feelings 4
  avoiding xvi
  suppressing xvi
fitness xiii
flight, fight or freeze response 7
flight to Sydney 44–45

G

goals 11–14
'good' habits xiv
guilt xiv, 96

H

habits xi–xviii, xv, 5, 25–26
  establishing xiii
  maintaining xiii–xv
  the problem with xii–xvi
habituation 25–26
happiness 10–11, 49
Hawkins, David 37, 50–53
holidays xiii
how we interact with the world xix–15
human mind 37
human senses 6, 26–29
hydrogen atoms 18–19

I

impermanence 9–11, 15, 22
imposter syndrome 85–86
inkblot test 45–46
inner force xiii–xv
  oppressing xiv
internal drives xii

J

Jha, Amish 47
journalling 7
Jung, Carl xv–xvi, 88

L

language
  limitations of 23–24
living in choice 107–109
love 23–24

M

Mackay, Hugh 64
making the unconscious conscious 13–14, 40
maladaptive behaviours xi
managing money 91–94
Melissa 32–33
memories 40, 98–99
memory erasing 98–101
Men in Black 98–101
messages from our body xv–xvi
metal stability xvi–xvii
Mindset Mastery
  definition of xvi–xviii
  in action 57–105, 107–109
muscle sensations 28

N

negotiating 21–22
non-attachment 11–14, 48–49
not reacting xiii, 8

O

observing 70–71

P

peace 5
perception 53
pornography 64
positive mental attitude xvi–xvii
possessing 66–67
post-traumatic stress disorder (PTSD) 9
predictable patterns of behaviour 5
prisoners of habit xi–xviii
procrastination 21–22
programming xv–xvi, xvii
  deactivating 8
projecting meaning 46–47
public speaking 24–25, 72
punishment 51, 52

R

rational actor 38
reacting xvii, 7–8, 14, 80–105
  from habit 5
  recognising 6–7
refractory period 8–9
regret xiv, 3
relaxing 4, 90–91
rewards 51
right and wrong 51, 53

Rorschach, Herman 45

S

sales calls xiii–xvii, 86–88
self-help books xi–xv, xvii
sensations *see* energetic sensations
sensory – body feedback loop 6–8, 14–15, 20–21, 37, 39, 64, 67
  observing 29–30
sex 64
Six Don'ts 13, 30, 71–74, 80–105
skin sensations 27
sleep 95–96
social media use xiii, 68
Stoics xv
stories 43–56
  sensations and 50–54
  value of 47–49
  whingers and 50–56
struggle between good and evil xii
suffering 9–12, 52
suppressing 65

T

television xiii–xix, 64
therapists 7

thoughts 4–5, 7–9, 12–13, 29–30, 37–39
   deactivating 42
   ignoring 13
   sensations and 38–39
   stopping 73–74
time travelling 40–41
trauma 9, 100
triggering events xvi–xvii, 8
truth 51–52

U

understanding your programming 1–15
unhappiness 10–11

V

victims xi
voice in your head 30–42

W

waking up in the morning 4
weight loss 94–95
whingers 19–21, 38
   stories and 50–56
willpower xiii–xv
winning 53
worrying 66

Y

you 2.0 101–103

ABOUT THE AUTHOR

Darren Fleming is a behavioural scientist and peak performance strategist. He is obsessed with helping people get the most from their mind and brain. He has qualifications in psychology and neuro-linguistic programming (NLP). He has worked for small family-run businesses, multinational corporations as well as ASX-listed companies and the Australian Public Service. A former International Athlete (sailing), he has seen what it takes to succeed in sport and business at the top level.

Darren helps clever people quieten the voice in their head so they can focus on what needs to be done without distractions taking them off task. He speaks at conferences, trains teams and coaches senior leaders so they can do less and achieve more. He has clients in Australia and all around the world.

You can reach him on:

@ darren@darrenfleming.com.au

🌐 www.darrenfleming.com.au

in www.linkedin.com/in/darrenfleming/

OTHER BOOKS BY DARREN FLEMING

Speak, Motivate, Lead: How real leaders inspire others to follow

The Secrets of Highly Effective Speakers

How to Write a 10-Minute Presentation in Under 2 Minutes

More Sales, More Profit – because that's what we all want

Don't be a Dick: Creating connections that make influence happen

Selling for Accountants

MINDSET MASTERY – THE PODCAST

Hear interviews on how business people, Olympians, psychologists and others deal with the pressures of mastering their mindset on the Mindset Mastery podcast. Just search for 'Darren Fleming Mindset Mastery' from your podcast provider.

MINDSET MASTERY PROGRAMS

If you're interested in having a conversation about enabling your team to do less and achieve more, visit **www.darrenfleming.com.au/mindset-mastery** to learn more. Otherwise, you can send an email to **darren@darrenfleming.com.au**.

ADDITIONAL RESOURCES

To access additional resources to help you implement the Mindset Mastery methodology into your life, simply visit **www.darrenfleming.com.au/mmresources**.
There you will find:

- A clickable reference list to access the all the books and papers referenced in this book.
- The *Six Don'ts* poster.
- Mindset Mastery Accelerator – an easy 5-step program to accelerate your success applying Mindset Mastery in your life.

www.ingramcontent.com/pod-product-compliance
Lightning Source LLC
Chambersburg PA
CBHW020425010526
44118CB00010B/429